Waiting in Joyful Hope

Daily Reflections for
Advent and Christmas 2005–2006
Year B

Katherine L. Howard, O.S.B.

LITURGICAL PRESS

Collegeville, Minnesota

www.litpress.org

ISSN 1550-803X

ISBN-13: 978-0-8146-2987-1
ISBN-10: 0-8146-2987-3

Introduction

From the beginning of the liturgical year we clearly express what is at the heart of the life of believers, the church, and the liturgy: the ardent desire for God and God's reign, the hope for the return of the Christ who is already present among his own, what waiting for the Lord's coming means for each believer, and the absolute need for the Spirit to fulfill our hope lest it be in vain.

Waiting may, in fact, be intolerable if there is no certainty of God's faithfulness, and if we do not know that the one who must come has already come. But we must not give up hoping. We are sure of God, of course, but we are also conscious of all the perils, interior and exterior, that beset us!

In evoking the centuries that preceded Christ, that is, by recalling in the liturgy the ancient oracles of a bygone era, the church is not inviting us to return to the past or to act as if Christ has not yet come. But it does remind us that at the end of Advent we celebrate what is not merely the birth of the Lord, but rather an event that happened once, and for all time, so that we might enjoy today the grace it generated.

The experience of ancient Israel still has meaning for today. The desire for God is never completely fulfilled here. The fullness of salvation overwhelms our capacity to receive it: we never cease being open to the immensity of the gift that has been given to us. Known and recognized as it is, however, God's love yet dwells in a hidden place. Furthermore, as we perceive God's wonders, we realize that we have scarcely seen anything, that we still have everything to discover. The temptations that assail our abiding hope do not alter its genuine nature or diminish its strength.

In celebrating the Eucharist Christians experience the sacrament of the presence of the Lord in the midst of a people now holy. But we are no less open to a gift that is yet to come (Latin, *advenire*), given our faith in what has already come *(adventum)*.*

May the Word of God, along with these thoughts, prayers, and reflections, help you to know more deeply what God has already done and is doing in your life, and may you yearn for what is to come.

---

* These paragraphs are taken and adapted from *Days of the Lord*, vol. 1 (Collegeville: Liturgical Press, 1991) 24, 31–32. *Days of the Lord* is a translation of *Jours du Seigneur*.

FIRST WEEK OF ADVENT

Be Alert

Readings: Isa 63:16b-17, 19b; 64:2-7; 1 Cor 1:3-9; Mark 13:33-37

Scripture:
Jesus said to his disciples:
"Be watchful! Be alert!
You do not know when the time will come." (Mark 13:33)

Reflection: The "time" Jesus is speaking about in today's gospel calls to mind that *"day of the LORD"* (Amos 5:18a, for example) referred to by the Old Testament prophets, the day on which the goodness and justice of God would definitively triumph over evil, the day when there would be peace in the land, harmony in the human family and all of creation. For those who were unprepared, it would be an experience of "darkness and not light" (Amos 5:18c). In the verses preceding the ones read today, Jesus equates this final coming of God with his own return, that is, the return of the Son of Man in glory (see Mark 13:26). Advent is about being watchful and alert as we eagerly look forward to *that day*. In every Mass we acclaim our faith and joyful anticipation of the return of the Son of Man when we declare during the Eucharistic Prayer, "Christ has died, Christ is risen, Christ will come again!" Or, "Dying you destroyed our death, rising you restored our life, Lord Jesus, come again in glory!"

It is difficult, though, to be on the lookout for that final coming, if we have not gotten into the habit of watching for Christ in his daily comings. Keeping vigil for Christ's coming may be most difficult during times of growing or complete inner darkness, the evenings and midnights of life. We are tempted to give up hope that Christ can or will come. We feel keenly the absence of God.

But Christ's coming, like the dawn, our faith tells us, can break through even our darkest hours; and in his light even the light of the sun will pale. In our patience through the darkness we have the spiritual strength to stay alert and wait for the dawn of his coming in whatever way that may take place now and in the future. "[F]or," as Paul reassures us, "the grace of God [has been] bestowed on [us] in Christ Jesus . . . so that [we] are not lacking in any spiritual gift as [we] wait for the revelation of our Lord Jesus Christ" (1 Cor 1:4-7).

Meditation: In what ways do you stay alert watching for the coming of Christ in the "evenings" and "nights" of your life? In what ways have you experienced the dawn of Christ's coming in the midst of darkness?

Prayer: O God of darkness and light, you come into our nights and days in Christ your Son. Keep us watchful and alert for the dawn of his presence each day so that we may welcome him when he comes in our final hour and at the end of time. Amen.

The Coming of God

Readings: Isa 2:1-5; Matt 8:5-11

Scripture:
When [Jesus] entered Capernaum,
  a centurion approached him and appealed to him saying,
  "Lord, my servant is lying at home paralyzed, suffering
    dreadfully."
He said to him, "I will come and cure him." (Matt 8:5-7)

Reflection: Jesus assures the worried Roman centurion that he will come and cure his son, though in the end the centurion's faith in the power of Jesus' healing word precludes the necessity of his actual physical presence with the sick child! It is Jesus' nature as God to be the one who comes to heal and save. From their first conscious experience of God the Israelites knew the divine as a compassionate and healing presence. God appeared to Moses in the burning bush saying: "I have witnessed the affliction of my people in Egypt and have heard their cry of complaint against their slave drivers, so I know well what they are suffering. Therefore I have come down to rescue them" (Exod 3:7-8a). In the gospels Jesus demonstrates the coming of this divine compassion and saving power in his words and actions.

God's coming to us in Jesus is the depth dimension of every event of our lives. The long anticipated arrival of a beloved spouse, daughter, son, or friend returning from a trip; the birth of a child . . . the rising of the sun after several days of darkness . . . the appearance of desperately needed help at the scene of an accident . . . the start of spring after a long winter . . . all these daily advents (comings) echo and embody the divine coming in the depths of our being and lives. When the smile of a stranger lifts our spirits, when the love of a spouse restores our energy, when peace arises from within in times of trouble, when a word of Scripture strengthens our soul, when the laugh of a child brings joy to our hearts, God is there in Jesus touching us with divine love and healing, with divine saving power.

During Advent we celebrate the coming of God to be lovingly with us, to help and heal us. It is the season to reflect on and affirm God's coming in Christ in the past and to refine our capacity to be aware of God's coming in Christ each day so that we can look forward in joy to that coming in Christ in glory at the end of our lives and the end of time.

Meditation: Recall some specific way God has come into your life in a healing way. What prayer arises in you out of that experience?

Prayer: Gracious God, you are the one who comes to heal and save, to bring joy and peace. Please help us see, hear, feel, understand the ways you are coming in Christ to heal and save us, to bring joy and peace so that we may be a channel of your coming to others in Christ your Son. Amen.

Stumps and Shoots

Readings: Isa 11:1-10; Luke 10:21-24

Scripture:
  On that day,
A shoot shall sprout from the stump of Jesse,
  and from his roots a bud shall blossom.
The Spirit of the LORD shall rest upon him:
  a Spirit of wisdom and of understanding,
A Spirit of counsel and of strength,
  a Spirit of knowledge and of fear of the LORD,
  and his delight shall be the fear of the LORD. (Isa 11:1-3a)

Reflection: There is an old azalea stump in my flowerpot that looks dead to me, but I am watering it—every day looking for a shoot, some new life to come from its roots. Speaking in the eight century B.C.E. the prophet Isaiah proclaimed confidently that even though King David's family tree, which had its roots in his father Jesse, was looking rather like a dead stump, it would give life to a green sprout that would blossom. Still a wonderful new shoot would come from that wasted stump. Filled with the Spirit of God that living branch would blossom finally in peace not only for Israel but for all nations, a peace brought about through the Messiah, that is, the Christ. (The Greek word *christos* translates the Hebrew *messiah*.)

That promised messianic reign of justice and peace has come in Christ Jesus whose words to his disciples in today's gospel are his words to us: "Blessed are the eyes that see what you see" (Luke 10:23). Out of years of fidelity to God in circumstances that often seemed like total disaster for Israel, Christ Jesus has come to earth as one of us and remains with us.

But you don't have to look far to know that the fullness of God's reign in Christ has not yet permeated our world. Yet, with the eyes of faith we catch glimpses of shoots and sprouts: the varied ways "Christ rejoices in the Spirit" within and around us. Tuning into those blessed manifestations of peace and harmony in our lives can sustain our hope when we begin to feel overwhelmed by the seemingly dead stumps in our world. In Christ the messianic reign has begun. Even that azalea may bloom again!

Meditation: Where have you seen manifestations of harmony and peace in your life over the last few days or weeks? How have you experienced the joy of the Spirit echoing in your life?

Prayer: Christ Jesus, you who are coming into our lives through the power of your Holy Spirit, open us more deeply to the influence of the gifts of your Spirit—gifts of knowledge and understanding, wisdom and counsel, strength, reverence, and love, so that together with all your people we may help bring about your reign of peace in the world. Amen.

Good News

Readings: Rom 10:9-18; Matt 4:18-22

Scripture:
For one believes with the heart and so is justified,
  and one confesses with the mouth and so is saved.
    (Rom 10:10)

Reflection: At one time or another you have probably felt the searing fingers of shame clutching at your heart and maybe even showing in the burning sensation of your blushed face. Such a simple thing as making a social error, perhaps giving the wrong name to someone you were introducing, may have left you wanting to disappear into the woodwork or through the floor! Most (if not all) of us have known that kind of embarrassment. However, there is a shame that exists at an even deeper level of our experience as a feeling of personal inadequacy. Usually this develops early in life as we internalize negative judgments and condemnations for our failures or seeming failures to measure up—whether that be emotionally, intellectually, physically, socially, or interpersonally. It is a paralyzing embarrassment at being who we are, just as we are.

Though the more superficial and circumstantial feelings of shame may never disappear completely from our lives, our faith in Christ assures us that at the deepest level, in the core of our being, we will never "be put to shame" (Rom 10:11). The Good News that Jesus came to preach and teach, and that the apostle Andrew continued to proclaim, is that belief in Christ makes us children of God, sharing God's life in the Spirit. In Christ our faith in all the original goodness of our created being is restored. We do measure up because we live in Christ, and Christ lives in us. Whatever our human foibles and unintended, inadvertent mistakes, we are in our deepest being good and lovable, and capable of loving others. Even sin, that is, our intentional failures to love ourselves and others, cannot permanently put us to shame. God's forgiveness in Christ opens us again and again to the healing Spirit of the risen Christ within us.

Opening our hearts—the center, the core of our being—to be embraced and to embrace the risen Christ in love can free us from the shame that paralyzes us and keeps us from loving others.

Meditation: What, if anything, about yourself and your life arouses shame? Intentionally open your inner being and entrust yourself with these particular characteristics to the divine goodness and mercy.

Prayer: God of all goodness, you sent Christ to proclaim the Good News of our salvation. Through the intercession of Saint Andrew and all the apostles may we be transformed by that good news—your incarnate Word who lives in us, and in whom we live and breathe. Amen.

A House on Rock

Readings: Isa 26:1-6; Matt 7:21, 24-27

Scripture:
Jesus said to his disciples:

. . . .

"Everyone who listens to these words of mine and acts
   on them
will be like a wise man who built his house on rock."
   (Matt 7:24)

Reflection: Building a house on the sand of a riverbank—
or a lake or seashore—is not a great idea. The people of
Palestine in Jesus' time knew this from experience. When
the spring rains came and streams rose up over the banks
of the riverbeds and swirled along they would wash away
any structure not founded on solid rock.

Today's gospel reading is the final section from the first
of Matthew's five discourses, the one known as the Sermon
on the Mount. The eight Beatitudes are the keynote of that
sermon. In the Beatitudes Jesus challenges the ways we
look for happiness by teaching that true joy comes only
when we are willing to embrace our poverty, to mourn our
losses and move on, to be gentle, authentically good and
merciful, to sift and let go of our self-centered motivations
and become pure in heart, to take our place among peace-

makers in the world, and to be willing to suffer whatever persecution a life based in these values brings (see Matt 5:1-10). In the conclusion of that sermon addressed to us in today's gospel, Jesus emphasizes that listening to the words of this discourse is not enough. Even understanding them deeply is not enough; only carrying them out, acting on them, can assure our lasting stability in the reign of God.

Living out this eightfold challenge to transform our lives and become firmly established in God's reign is to build our house on rock. But we cannot do it by ourselves. God is the chief builder, the one who "sets up walls and ramparts to protect us" (Isa 26:1c), as we are assured in today's first reading. In fact, God not only is the builder, but also is the "eternal Rock" (Isa 26:4b) on which our house, our being, our life rests. If we trust God, the foundation of our life, to guide our choices and bring our actions to fulfillment, we will not be washed away.

Meditation: In what way are you presently being asked to act on Christ's word in your life? With humility, simplicity, and confidence, ask for God's help.

Prayer: Faithful God, our eternal Rock, open the ears of our hearts to your Word in our lives today. Guide our choices and give us the courage and stamina to live and act in harmony with the teaching and life of your Word, Jesus Christ, so that firmly established in your divine reign we may live with you now and forever. This we ask in Christ's name through the power of the Holy Spirit. Amen.

On That Day

Readings: Isa 29:17-24; Matt 9:27-31

Scripture:
As Jesus passed by, two blind men followed him,
    crying out,
    "Son of David, have pity on us!" (Matt 9:27)

Reflection: There are many ways to be blind. The physical lack of sight suffered by the two blind men in today's gospel is a metaphor for our own blindness, our spiritual blindness. Though the light of God is shining in our world and our lives, we cannot see it unless the inner eyes of our spirit are equipped to receive the light that comes from God.

Before the inventions of the telescope and the microscope we were blind to many distant planets and stars and to many nearby creatures that we can see now with the help of these instruments. Only recently have I heard about the "M theory" physicists and mathematicians have been excitedly working on during the last decade or so as an explanation of the origin, basic nature, and scope of the universe. Even though it is way beyond my understanding, I am intrigued by its suggestion that there may be eleven dimensions to physical reality. With our natural eyes we see only three. Perhaps the ingenuity and creativity of the human mind may come up with instruments to attune our eyes to these other dimensions of our existence to which we are currently blind.

Our world, whether three or eleven dimensional, has another facet: its divine dimension. God is not geographically distant from us and our universe. From the Letter to the Colossians we know that "in [Christ] were created all things in heaven and on earth . . . / [A]nd in him all things hold together" (Col 1:16a, 17b). Christ, the Son of God is the divine dimension that lights up our world and our lives. However, we cannot see this dimension with our physical eyes, not even with the help of glasses or scopes. This kind of sight is possible only for our inner, spiritual eyes. These inner eyes, too, need to be properly equipped—with faith—in order to receive this light that comes from God. That is why with the two blind men today we earnestly cry out, "Son of David, have pity on us!" (Matt 9:27b).

Meditation: In what areas of your life would you like to have more faith in the presence of Christ? Close your eyes and pray in the words of the blind men.

Prayer: Jesus, Son of David and Son of God, you are the spiritual light of our lives and our universe, open our inner eyes in faith so that seeing you we may spread the Good News of your constant coming

The Reign of God

Readings: Isa 30:19-21, 23-26; Matt 9:35–10:1, 5a, 6-8

Scripture:
Jesus sent out these twelve after instructing them thus,
   "Go to the lost sheep of the house of Israel.
As you go, make this proclamation: 'The Kingdom of
   heaven is at hand.'
Cure the sick, raise the dead,
   cleanse lepers, drive out demons.
Without cost you have received; without cost you are to
   give." (Matt 10:5a, 6-8)

Reflection: Today's gospel reading joins Matthew's sum-
mary of Jesus' healing ministry to the beginning of his
second great discourse, the one on the church's mission.
Matthew asserts that when Jesus went about to all the towns
proclaiming the Good News of God's reign he cured "every
disease and illness" (9:35). The second part of today's gospel
shows Jesus entrusting the proclamation of God's reign to
the twelve apostles, those sent to carry out his mission.
   There are countless places in which the prophets speak
of the future time in which God's rule will prevail. This day
of the coming of the reign of God is the one in which God,
the Holy One, will be in Israel's midst as the source of peace,
harmony, abundance, and well-being. As God says in the

poetic words of Isaiah that we hear today, it will be a time when there is no more weeping, when rain, rich soil, fertile pasturelands, and prospering flocks abound—a time when God's people will know the divine presence.

In the historical Jesus the reign of God was among us clothed in our humanity. Jesus' words proclaimed this good news and his healing actions demonstrated it. God's reign continues in our midst in his risen presence through the power of Christ's Holy Spirit. Why then are we having all this trouble? People are still weeping! Violence abounds! God often seems absent! Our experience tells us that God's reign is not yet complete! But our faith in the Good News assures us not only that God's reign is here, but that we have a part in bringing it to completion. Today Jesus is calling us as his apostles in our contemporary world to spread the good news of God's reign, not just in words but through lives that manifest healing, peace, forgiveness, generosity, consolation, and hope for life eternal.

Meditation: In what ways are you being invited to bring the Good News of God's healing power into the world?

Prayer: Jesus, Healer of the Sick, thank you for the balm of your Spirit which has restored, strengthened, and comforted us through your faithful servants. Through the gifts of that same Holy Spirit help us as your disciples to bring your healing presence into the life of others. Amen.

SECOND WEEK OF ADVENT

December 4: Second Sunday of Advent

Repent

Readings: Isa 40:1-5, 9-11; 2 Pet 3:8-14; Mark 1:1-8

Scripture:
A voice cries out:
In the desert prepare the way of the LORD!
   Make straight in the wasteland a highway for our God!
Every valley shall be filled in,
   every mountain and hill shall be made low;
the rugged land shall be made a plain,
   the rough country, a broad valley. (Isa 40:3-4)

Reflection: Today John the Baptist is inviting us to repent. Repentance is also the theme Jesus took up when he began his ministry after John's arrest: "Repent, and believe in the gospel" (Mark 1:15c). In Jesus' language and culture it was common to use two expressions in a parallel fashion to express the same truth. To believe in the Gospel, Jesus was saying, was to repent. To repent is not to berate ourselves for our failures but to believe the good news that God's reign of love is here (Mark 1:15b). If we accept this love for ourselves just as we are, our hearts will be changed and able to extend God's goodness and acceptance to others.

God is always coming into our world in Christ, but it is not possible for that loving presence to permeate an inhospitable landscape. Isaiah recognizes that the 'place' we are preparing to welcome God is a "wasteland"—it needs a "highway." In its current condition it is too rough to be hospitable—not only too many potholes and bumps but too many mountains and valleys! This symbolic geography describes our world and our souls, misshapen with bumps and mountains of hatred and resentment, with potholes and valleys of fear and mistrust.

However, we do not have to be slaves to these inner, negative attitudes that hold us in their grip and control our outward behavior. Choosing, with God's grace, to believe in the reign of God within us makes it possible to let go of the fear and mistrust, the resentment and hatred that keep us from knowing God's love for us and manifesting that love for others.

Meditation: Take fifteen or twenty minutes today to settle down in a quiet place by yourself and open to your inner landscape, noticing what is going on without judgment. Accept one negative attitude you find there, then gently let it go by replacing it with an expression of your faith in God's reign within.

Prayer: Word of God, you continually announce the Good News of God's reign within and among us. Please strengthen our belief in that Good News so that freed from fear and mistrust, hatred and resentment, we may help you spread that reign. This we ask in your name. Amen.

Incredible Things

Readings: Isa 35:1-10; Luke 5:17-26

Scripture:
[The man who was paralyzed] stood up immediately before
    them,
    picked up what he had been lying on,
    and went home, glorifying God.
Then astonishment seized them all and they glorified God,
    and, struck with awe, they said,
    "We have seen incredible things today." (Luke 5:25-26)

Reflection: Incredibly wonderful things do happen every
day. The earth spins on its orbit around the sun fantasti-
cally fast, yet we do not fly off. We keep our bearings and
occasionally even stop to be still and at peace while still
moving at tremendous rates of speed. Irrigation turns deserts
into fertile fields, restoration projects replenish drained
wetlands, miracle drugs cure diseases, a loved one returns
to us from the gates of death. Some of us at least have seen
some strides toward international peace: the Berlin Wall
coming down, former enemy nations becoming friends.

But Jesus announces the most incredible event in today's
gospel when he says to the paralytic, "As for you, your sins
are forgiven" (Luke 5:20b). He is claiming the divine power
to release the paralyzed man—and us—from opposition to

other human beings and opposition to God. Jesus opens within us the capacity to love with the unconditional love of God.

Our sins are the destructive things we do to ourselves and others to satisfy our excessive, sometimes desperate, and most often unconscious drives for security, for affection and esteem, for power and control. These drives have developed in all of us as we grew into full human self-consciousness without basic needs being satisfied—or with the perception that they were not. Physical paralysis seems a good symbol for the inner condition that comes from these excessive drives. Jesus responds to desire for healing by awakening in the paralytic God's unconditional love. Jesus does the same for the paralysis in each of us.

Meditation: What inner obstacle separates you from God or another? With faith in God's unconditional love present in Jesus, open your mind and heart to that person and listen over and over again to these words addressed to you: "As for you, your sins are forgiven" (Luke 5:20b).

Prayer: God of unconditional love, your wonders have not ceased. You are still the God who is coming to save us in Christ Jesus. Free us from those obstacles that keep us blind, and deaf, separated from one another and you, so that we may spread your peace in our world and sing together forever in your eternal home. Amen.

December 6: Tuesday of the Second Week of Advent

Comfort and Care

Readings: Isa 40:1-11; Matt 18:12-14

Scripture:
Like a shepherd he feeds his flock;
    in his arms he gathers the lambs,
Carrying them in his bosom,
    and leading the ewes with care. (Isa 40:11)

Reflection: Have you ever seen a tall, muscular father cradle a newborn in his arms holding it gently against his chest? Or a strong, young mother caressing her baby tenderly at her breast? These images are like the shepherd who "gathers the lambs, / Carrying them in his bosom" (Isa 40:11). Every time I read or hear this passage, the liquid, gently undulating melody of the alto air that carries these words in Handel's oratorio, *Messiah*, echoes within me. I slow down, stop, and am again amazed and grateful for this call back into the deepest reality of our existence: God, the Good Shepherd, is carrying each of us in strong and gentle arms.

We, of course, are now adults who are called to be manifestations of God's strong love for others: our spouses, children, elderly parents and grandparents, needy neighbors, the poor of our cities and states, colleagues at work, sick and suffering relatives and friends. The enduring strength we need to be there for others daily, however, is not something we can muster up purely by willpower. When we try that we usually, if not always, end up depleted, resentful, unable, and unwilling. We ourselves need to be regularly nurtured, fed, carried. Often this nurturing comes through our spouses, parents, sisters and brothers, neighbors, friends. But if we and they are going to make it over the long haul, we need time regularly to let go and entrust ourselves to the Good Shepherd who "feeds," and "gathers" us, "Carrying [us] in his bosom" (Isa 40:11). We need time for resting in the limitless abundance of divine energy that God pours out from within and around us.

In the gospel reading Christ, the Good Shepherd, reassures us that even when we are lost—confused, frightened, separated from others and even from ourselves—God will find us, pick us up, and carry us home. Because that divine mercy and compassion sustains us in our weakness and need, we have the capacity to extend it to the little ones in our midst (see Matt 18:10, 14).

Meditation: Listen several times to the air "He shall feed his flock," from Handel's *Messiah*, or some other comforting music. Let it touch your soul and rest in its peace.

Prayer: Good and loving Shepherd, thank you for including me and all your people in the flock that you are gathering together. Please continue to feed us and carry us in our weakness so that growing strong with your power, we may assist you in finding and caring for each other. Amen.

December 7: Wednesday of the Second Week of Advent

Rest for the Weary

Readings: Isa 40:25-31; Matt 11:28-30

Scripture:
[God] does not faint nor grow weary,
. . . .
[God] gives strength to the fainting;
. . . .
Though young men faint and grow weary,
   and youths stagger and fall,
They that hope in the LORD will renew their strength,
   they will soar as with eagles' wings;
They will run and not grow weary,
   walk and not grow faint. (Isa 40:28c-31)

Reflection: About twenty years ago I ran in a few marathons. When I had trained well and found the right pace, I enjoyed the first sixteen to eighteen miles or so without fainting or growing weary (see Isa 40:28c). After that even the flattest courses were uphill in my mind and body! Others around me—even some younger than I was—women and men, were "staggering and falling" (see Isa 40:30), if not to the ground, at least to the sidelines and long before the finish. And by mile eighteen I had "hit the wall."

Life's course is as much or more a marathon than these road races. Even when we train well by developing and living a healthy physical, emotional, and spiritual life, and even when we set a reasonable pace, those "mile eighteens" come with sometimes steep inclines and rough terrain that leave us physically, emotionally, and spiritually winded.

God does not expect us "to pull ourselves up by the bootstraps" and push on without help but says "Stop trying so hard to do it yourself; put your hope in me and I will renew your strength."

To place our "hope in the LORD" (Isa 40:31) is first of all to let go of our expectations that we will be able to manage all life's problems, control its outcomes, achieve all the material, personal, relational, and career goals we set out after. As we work our way through the suffering these seeming setbacks bring, we may begin to see how failures, tragedies, disappointments, forced changes in plans and directions are graced invitations to shift our hope more completely to God. We learn that we can come to Jesus with the weariness of our limitations and the burden of our suffering. Accepting these in union with Jesus in his humbleness of heart brings us the rest that renews and sustains us.

Meditation: Write down the burdens that are too much for you to carry by yourself. Close your eyes, sit back, and give them to Jesus in a few words, or breathe them out slowly with each breath. Breathe in God's renewing strength. Rest.

Prayer: Jesus, in our exhaustion help us humbly entrust you with our weariness and burdens. Please give the rest and renewed strength we need for our lives of service. Amen.

December 8: Solemnity of the Immaculate Conception
(Roman Catholic Church)

Thursday of the Second Week of Advent
(Episcopal Church)

Mary

Readings: Gen 3:9-15, 20; Eph 1:3-6, 11-12; Luke 1:26-38

Scripture:
Then the angel said to her,
  "Do not be afraid, Mary,
  for you have found favor with God." (Luke 1:30)

Reflection: The conception identified in the title of this feast is that of Mary, not Jesus. Graced by God, Mary was free from original sin. That means that from the first moment of her existence in her mother Anne's womb, Mary was completely free from any obstacles to God's work in her. The instant the love of Anne and Joachim brought Mary into being, her body-soul-spirit was resonating in full harmony with God's will. She was the earthly instrument perfectly attuned to the Great Artist, the Spirit of God, who would later invite her cooperation in composing and premiering that new song of creation—God's becoming one with humanity in Jesus. Today we celebrate the wonderful mystery of Mary's total openness to God from the moment she began to come into being.

Through the sexual union of Anne and Joachim, and of their countless ancestors, and through Mary's and her parents' own natural ties to the land of their birth—its mountains and hills, rivers and rugged desert, its fertile plains—Mary's being was deeply rooted in the earth. And in Mary, because of God's special grace, earth was fully accessible to heaven, that is, to the divine life. As a single, pregnant woman in her culture Mary would have had no security, no esteem from others, no future to anticipate with worldly confidence. Yet because of her grace-filled bodily being, Mary was not bound by fear, self-interest, convention, or precedents. She had the courage, freedom, willingness, and ability to risk giving the full-hearted "Yes!" that allowed Divine Love to wed heaven and earth in her womb.

Meditation: Imagine Mary as the flowering of earth's original goodness and beauty, fully open to God's will. Invite her into your presence, addressing her with names and titles that express the richness and loveliness of that grace-filled flowering.

Prayer: O Mary, greenest bough, exquisite blossom, supple branch, intercede for us with God. Pray that we, your earthly sisters and brothers, drawn into the stream of your graced life, may live in blessed harmony with God's will. Amen.

God as Teacher

Readings: Isa 48:17-19; Matt 11:16-19

Scripture:
I, the LORD, your God,
    teach you what is for your good,
    and lead you on the way you should go.
If [only] you would hearken to my commandments.
    (Isa 48:17)

Reflection: Most of us have many teachers during our lifetime. Some of them touch us at a profound level in ways that change our lives for the better. Their positive influence often comes through loving acceptance, compassionate understanding, and genuine appreciation of our uniqueness and particular abilities. Students whose teachers believe in and respect their ability to learn do much better than those whose teachers think their learning capacity is very limited. Of course, a teacher could be the best in the world and still, if a student remains unwilling to open her heart she will not learn.

Today's first reading assures us that God is with us as the good, respectful, and caring teacher who knows what we need to learn and is leading us surely on our life's path. Because God knows us through and through, understands all our thoughts, is familiar with all our ways (see Psalm 139),

God can guide us with certainty. We, however, must listen and respond. That is not always easy, especially because God rarely, if ever, speaks to us in words that resound in our ears. Sometimes you may, like me, find yourself saying: "Could you speak louder, please. I am a little hard of hearing!" The problem with our hearing may not be God's voice but our own ears. God is speaking in many ways in our lives—through local, national, and world events; through our own insights, feelings, intuitions, and interior inspirations of the Spirit; through the words and actions of others with whom we live and work; and through the words of Scripture and liturgy.

To hear our Divine Teacher in any one or any combination of these places we need to be able to listen attentively with both our outer and inner ears, something we can do only if we are silent.

Meditation: Recall a significant episode in your life when your choice to be silent and let go of a judgment about a person, a group of people, or an event opened your inner ear to a word from God. What judgments and controls are stopping up your ears today?

Prayer: Divine Teacher, give us the grace to stop our incessant chatter and to give up our efforts to judge and control everything and everyone in our lives. In silence help us hear your guiding voice in the multiple and varied ways you speak to us in daily life. This we ask through Jesus Christ in the power of the Holy Spirit. Amen.

December 10: Saturday of the Second Week of Advent

Reconciliation

Readings: Sir 48:1-4, 9-11; Matt 17:9a, 10-13

Scripture:
How awesome are you, Elijah, in your wondrous deeds!
. . . .
You were destined, it is written, in time to come
　to put an end to wrath before the day of the LORD.
To turn back the heart of fathers toward their sons,
　and to re-establish the tribes of Jacob. (Sir 48:4a, 10)

Reflection: Reconciliation, putting an end to hatred and divisions between family members, friends, and within and between nations, races, and religions is a daunting task. It takes some breakthrough of grace! There have been and continue to be many instances of that grace at work.

The South African Truth and Reconciliation Commission established by Nelson Mandela, for example, made it possible for victims of apartheid to make public the atrocities committed against them, and for their oppressors to admit guilt and seek forgiveness. This process carried out over several years time, though it did not solve all problems, made possible a relatively peaceful transition to a society in which blacks and whites were by law, at least, considered equal.

The Straight Story, a 1999 film written by John Roach and Mary Sweeney, and directed by David Lynch, depicts reconciliation between two brothers. In it elderly, cantankerous Alvin Straight who hadn't spoken to his brother in ten years, with much effort and overcoming many obstacles, rides his lawn mower, his only means of transportation, from Laurens, Iowa, to Mount Zion, Wisconsin, to make amends with his brother Lyle. He had come to the realization that "whatever it was that made me and Lyle so mad . . . doesn't matter to me now . . . I want to make peace . . . I want to sit with him again and look up at all the stars" (*The Straight Story,* © 1999 The Straight Story, Inc. and Walt Disney Pictures).

The grace that moved Nelson Mandela and the participants in the work of the South African Truth and Reconciliation Commission, and the grace that touched Alvin and Lyle Straight is ours too, for the asking.

Meditation: Bring to mind and imagination someone with whom you want to be reconciled. Invite Jesus to join you. Ask him to give you the willingness, courage, and whatever else you need to take the initiative to reach out to that person.

Prayer: Jesus, you who have reconciled us to God by becoming one of us and sharing our lot, please open our hearts and help us find ways to reconnect with those from whom we are alienated. This we pray trusting in you. Amen.

THIRD WEEK OF ADVENT

Make Straight God's Way

Readings: Isa 61:1-2a, 10-11; 1 Thess 5:16-24; John 1:6-8, 19-28

Scripture:
A man named John was sent from God.
. . . .
He said:
> "I am *the voice of one crying out in the desert,*
> *make straight the way of the Lord,*
> as Isaiah the prophet said." (John 1:6, 23)

Reflection: Our baptism is not just a once-in-a-lifetime ritual. Our descent into the waters of Christ's dying, and our rising out of their depths filled with the life of Christ's Spirit is an ongoing event. It immerses us continually in the life of Christ—the spiritual dimension of our existence. But Christ cannot act in and through us unless we attune our bodies, souls, and spirits to his presence and action within us. St. Paul gives us some ways to do that: "Rejoice," "Pray," be grateful. Don't put out the fire of the Spirit. Listen for the prophets among you. Be willing to try new ways of thinking and acting, then evaluate them keeping what is good! (see 1 Thess 5:16-22).

Because of the life of the Spirit within us, we do have the inner freedom to turn our attention away from life-sapping thoughts of gloom and doom so the joy of the Spirit can bubble up. We can make choices to let go of negative or useless thoughts, turning rather to some short expression of prayer. We can make it a point to remember everyday to be grateful for something good—the breath of life, the chance to work, the love of a friend, some hoped for reconciliation between individuals or groups. We can choose to listen to prophets who are speaking on behalf of the poor and oppressed for justice and peace. We can take some risks in connecting with our inner selves, with other people and cultures, finding some creative ways to unity and peace. If with the help of the Holy Spirit we do these things daily, we will be making God's way straight and we will "be preserved blameless for the coming of our Lord Jesus Christ" (1 Thess 5:23) in glory at the end of time.

Meditation: Sit down in a quiet place where you will be undisturbed for a little while; notice your breathing. Be aware of each thought as it comes but let each go as you repeat slowly and trustingly the phrase from today's responsorial psalm, "My soul rejoices in you, my God."

Prayer: Eternal Coming One, help us to prepare our hearts and minds to welcome you in Jesus, your Son who lives within us, and in whom we live. May our joy in him radiate in our lives so that others may rejoice in you. Amen.

December 12: Feast of Our Lady of Guadalupe
(Roman Catholic Church)

Tuesday of the Third Week of Advent
(Episcopal Church)

Nuestra Senora Guadalupe

Readings: Zech 2:14-17 or Rev 11:19a; 12:1-6a, 10ab;
Luke 1:26-38 or Luke 1:39-47

Scripture:
A great sign appeared in the sky, a woman clothed with
 the sun,
 with the moon under her feet,
 and on her head a crown of twelve stars. (Rev 12:1)

Reflection: Some friends of mine have a lovely ceramic tile rendition of Our Lady of Guadalupe set right over their kitchen sink among the plain blue tiles. Surrounded by the sun's rays, clothed in a mantle of stars, the crescent moon beneath her feet, she oversees and protects the cosmos as she lovingly watches over meal preparation, service and cleanup. She is right at home there—in both places. Her lovely brown skin identifies her with those of mixed race, simple peasants, the poor, the despised. The radiance of sun, stars, and moon proclaim her Queen of Heaven.

In 1531 at Tepeyac, Mexico, Mary appeared in a vision like that to Juan Diego, a poor, baptized native boy who was on his way to religious instructions. In 1999 John Paul II proclaimed Our Lady of Guadalupe patroness not just of Mexico, but of all the Americas. We South Americans and North Americans are one. We share a hemisphere of the earth. We have common blessings and common problems. Mary stands with us to protect and help us, especially the lowly and poor with whom she identifies. With Mary as our Mother, all of us are sisters and brothers: indigenous peoples, Latinos, Anglos, and all races and cultures that have come to claim some part of the Americas as home.

Meditation: Call to mind by face and name your neighbors, friends, associates of other races and cultures, particularly those from Mexico or other parts of Latin America. Entrust them and yourself to the loving care of Mary.

Prayer: Loving Mother of God and our Mother, continue to protect and help all of your people here in the Americas. Through your intercession may we grow in insight and compassion so that we may see and work untiringly for a just distribution of our rich resources among all your children who share this hemisphere of the earth. Amen.

Chief Priest and Elder, Tax Collector and Prostitute

Readings: Zeph 3:1-2, 9-13; Matt 21:28-32

Scripture:
Jesus said to them, "Amen, I say to you,
   tax collectors and prostitutes
   are entering the Kingdom of God before you.
When John came to you in the way of righteousness,
   you did not believe him;
   but tax collectors and prostitutes did. (Matt 21:31b-32a)

Reflection: Many of the religious leaders of Jesus' time looked down on the tax collectors and prostitutes. Yet these social and religious outcasts, Jesus says, not the religious leaders, were the ones who took John the Baptist's call to repentance seriously. These sinners, like the first son in the parable of today's gospel, by their immediate response to the law had said in effect, "No, I will not serve!" Yet when they heard the way of righteousness preached by John, they changed their minds. On the other hand, the religious elders Jesus is addressing here in Matthew's Gospel are like the son who said "Yes, I will go and work in the vineyard," but never showed up. By their words they were mouthing willingness to serve God, but they refused the deeper conversion to which John was inviting them. They did not even change their minds and believe John after they saw the sincere change of heart and quite amazing change of behavior by the tax collectors and prostitutes (see Matt 21:32).

This dynamic is at work in our relationship with God. Each of us is both chief priest or elder, and also tax collector or prostitute. We too may manage to mouth a superficial "yes" to the righteousness preached by John, but unless our lives and actions express a sincere and heartfelt willingness to welcome and live the Gospel in concrete ways in daily life, we will not enter the Kingdom of God. And sometimes when we realize what following the Gospel call means and say, "I just can't," we later find the energy of divine Love, and take up a generous and wholehearted service of God and neighbor in spite of our initial response. Today Jesus is commending and challenging us—commending the prostitute or tax collector within us who has often reversed that first negative response to God's invitation to love—and challenging that superficially upright part of us that says, "Yes, I'm willing to serve," but does not carry through.

Meditation: Recall a time when you were not really willing to serve, but said "Yes" and didn't show up. Recall a time when you said "No" but later had a change of heart.

Prayer: Faithful God, you know us in our rising and our falling. Through the Spirit of your Son, Jesus, who lives within us, strengthen our wills so that we may grow in our ability to respond honestly and generously to you. Amen.

Weariness and Doubt

Readings: Isa 45:6c-8, 18, 21c-25; Luke 7:18b-23

Scripture:
At that time,
John summoned two of his disciples and sent them to the
     Lord to ask,
  "Are you the one who is to come, or should we look for
     another?" (Luke 7:18b-19)

Reflection: Though we cannot know for sure what prompted John's sending disciples to ask Jesus whether he was "the one who was to come," the question itself seems to convey some honest doubt ("Well, it could be he is not really the one!"), some mental fatigue ("Maybe I should give up this search!"), even a little impatience ("Let's get this thing settled! I'm tired of this not knowing!"). It does not seem too far-fetched to imagine that John was uncertain and getting a bit weary about wondering just who it was for whom he was preparing the way! That uncertainty and weariness were part of his struggle to know who he himself was, and what his mission was supposed to accomplish!

John was probably looking around, watching for the return of Elijah whose fiery presence was to introduce the messianic age.

As Christians we ask ourselves or others: Am I in the right vocation, the right career? If I am, am I "doing it right?" Is this really the way God wants my life to go? Is this the person I should marry? Is this the vocation I should follow? In this place? Are you, God, here with me, or should I look someplace else, try some other route? Is all the energy, intelligence, time, effort I am putting into this project in accord with your will, or should I give it up and move in a different direction. Just please "put your cards on the table," give me some certainty.

Jesus' reply to John affirms his own identity as the fulfillment of the compassionate messianic promise of Isaiah. He does this by pointing out the fruit of his works: good news for the poor, healing for the sick, lifting up for the downtrodden (see Isa 61:1). In our own struggles with identity and purpose in life, and in the weariness and doubt such struggles bring, we can also look to those standards to help us assess the authenticity of our Christian identity and vocation.

Meditation: Who are you and how does your mission in life fit in with that of Jesus?

Prayer: O God of the poor, the sick, the downtrodden, you have come into our world in Jesus who shares with us the good news of your reign. Through the transforming power of your Holy Spirit please continue to shape my identity in his likeness so that I may carry out his mission. Amen.

With Enduring Love

Readings: Isa 54:1-10; Luke 7:24-30

Scripture:
For he who has become your husband is your Maker;
   his name is the LORD of hosts;
Your redeemer is the Holy One of Israel,
   called God of all the earth. (Isa 54:5)

Reflection: Every human heart longs for intimacy. We want to know and be known, to understand and be understood, to love and be loved at the deepest level of our being. We are fortunate if we find such intimacy in marriage, kinship, or friendship. Some do, some do not. Even if we do, that love, that intimacy can never totally fulfill our longing which is infinite, nor can such loves in their earthly form be unconditional or last forever. Even if the unpredictable circumstances of life do not intervene, death eventually changes things. At some time and in some measure or form we all suffer the grief of love betrayed, love lost, or love unrealized. Robert Frost in his poem "Reluctance" laments the passing of autumn as a metaphor for such experiences, capturing the deep sadness in his final verse:

    Ah, when to the heart of man
      Was it ever less than a treason

To go with the drift of things,
    To yield with a grace to reason,
And bow and accept the end
    Of a love or a season?

(*The Poetry of Robert Frost,* ed. Edward Connery Lathem [New York: Holt, Rinehart and Winston, 1969] 30)

Such sadness can lead to despair, but it can also be a channel to a deeper love and intimacy with God, and in God with others.

The Good News of today's liturgy is that God wants and is here offering an intimate loving relationship to each of us, a relationship rooted in the divine unconditional love and enduring fidelity. Though in our sadness and despair we may feel separated, or even choose to separate ourselves from God and others, our divine Lover whose nature is to be faithful continues to address us saying: "with great tenderness I will take you back," and "with enduring love I take pity on you" (Isa 54:7, 8). God our Creator, the "God of all the earth" does not stand far off, but God our Maker "has become [our spouse]" (Isa 54:5).

Meditation: Through what experiences of grief is the Divine Lover inviting you into a more intimate relationship?

Prayer: O Infinite Tenderness and Enduring Love, comfort us in our grief and sorrow. Let us know the intimate love you have for us in Christ Jesus, so that living in you with complete trust and confidence, we may spread your love in our world. Amen.

December 16: Friday of the Third Week of Advent

Salvation for All People

Readings: Isa 56:1-3a, 6-8; John 5:33-36

Scripture:
Let not the foreigner say,
> when he would join himself to the LORD,
> "The LORD will surely exclude me from his people."

The foreigners who join themselves to the LORD,
. . . .
Them I will bring to my holy mountain
> and make joyful in my house of prayer. (Isa 56:3a, 7a)

Reflection: A house is most often the center of our lives; it is our home. Our house expresses our personality, our spirit, our interests and connections. God's house is Christ, in whom, for whom, and through whom "all things are created" (Col 1:16), and the Holy Spirit who is the living love between Christ and the Father is the living Spirit of that house. All are welcome in the caring embrace of God.

Our sights, however, are sometimes set more narrowly. We are not so inclusive. We tend to think in terms of a duplex, if not an apartment complex, and we end up taking sides—our side and their side—with God on our side, living in our house! Of course, God *is* on our side.

But God's "our" does not have the same circumference as our "our"! We get caught in prejudices that come from over-identification with "our" neighborhood or city, "our" country, "our" parish, "our" religion, "our" race. God's "our" has no circumference at all; it is limitless.

We may wonder whether God can love those who deny God's very existence, or those who hate God, or hate a neighbor to the point of rejecting that person and refusing reconciliation to the grave. Can God love people who torture and abuse others, people who are unjust? Though it is hard to grasp and seems contrary to reason, the truth is that divine love does not withhold itself from anyone, even those who refuse to receive it. God is always inviting all of us to accept and turn back to the divine love and to live in harmony with it, observing "what is right," doing "what is just" and keeping our hands "from any evildoing" (Isa 56:1, 2). God's house is for everyone, and God never tires of inviting and welcoming us home.

Meditation: When you said "we" yesterday or today, who was included? Who excluded? Think or say "we" now, and open its circle to some you tend to exclude.

Prayer: God of all, you who invite each of your children into the limitless circle of your love, expand our hearts to welcome everyone who comes into our lives, people of every race, nation, gender, sexual orientation, religion, economic class. This we pray in Christ Jesus, brother to us all. Amen.

Wisdom's House

O Antiphon:
O Wisdom of our God Most High,
guiding creation with power and love:
come to teach us the path of knowledge!

Readings: Gen 49:2, 8-10; Matt 1:1-17

Scripture:
Boaz became the father of Obed,
whose mother was Ruth.

. . . .

David became the father of Solomon,
whose mother had been the wife of Uriah. (Matt 1:5b, 6b)

Reflection: Today the church begins to sing the O Antiphons before and after the *Magnificat* at Evening Prayer. The *Lectionary for Mass,* in the Roman Catholic communion, uses them as part of the Alleluia verse, before the gospel, for December 17–23. (That translation is used here.)

In the biblical book named after her, Wisdom is praised as "an aura of the might of God / and a pure effusion of the glory of the Almighty" (Wis 7:25).

Jesus' human genealogy clearly stems back to David and to Abraham, showing that Jesus is the Messiah, the Davidic king of Israel who will fulfill the promises first made to Abraham.

None of the women named in that genealogy fits the cultural norm for a Jewish wife and mother: Tamar, through deceit, entered into an incestuous union with her father-in-law Judah (see Gen 38). Rahab was a prostitute of Jericho who sheltered Hebrew spies (see Josh 2). Ruth was a foreigner who became part of the Israelite community because of her loyalty to her deceased husband's mother (see Ruth 1). Bathsheba was the partner of David's adultery (see 2 Sam 11). Mary was an unwed mother. It is important to note, however, that Tamar's deceit and incestuous union were the result of Judah's denying her a widow's right to marry the brother of her dead husband. The prostitution of Rahab was a part of what was seen as a legitimate trade, especially for women whose social status as orphans or widows deprived them of identity and livelihood. Bathsheba's adultery was the result of David's desire and power. And Mary's virginal motherhood was the work of God.

Wisdom lived in these women just as they were. Why would we ever doubt that in Christ Wisdom can and does live in us?

Meditation: Acknowledging the difficulties of your own life, invite Lady Wisdom to let you know her eternal light, power, and goodness living in you in Christ.

Prayer: *Sophia* God, you know the depths of our souls. Pour out the triumphant goodness of your self in us so that your incarnation in Christ may reach its completion in all of humanity. Amen.

FOURTH WEEK OF ADVENT

Houses

O Antiphon:
O Leader of the House of Israel,
giver of the Law to Moses on Sinai:
come to rescue us with your mighty power!

Readings: 2 Sam 7:1-5, 8b-12, 14a, 16; Rom 16:25-27;
Luke 1:26-38

Scripture:
The LORD also reveals to you
   that he will establish a house for you.
And when your time comes and you rest with your
      ancestors,
   I will raise up your heir after you, sprung from your
      loins,
   and I will make his kingdom firm. (2 Sam 7:11b-12)

Reflection: Much of life centers around houses: the house
that was our original home, the houses we moved to as we
grew up, the house we rented when we married and started
a family, the dream house we scrimped and saved for, the
scaled down retirement house we looked forward to. Adequate housing is difficult for many people in our society to
find. Thank God for "Habitat for Humanity," and groups

like it that work with people to provide good, affordable houses for homemaking.

The noun "house" has many definitions. That makes it possible for the author of 2 Samuel to use it in a very rich way, playing on those various meanings: a family home, a temple, a family lineage.

The gospel reading refers to the first house for God incarnate on our earth, that is, the womb of Mary. She who was a poor "handmaid of the Lord" (Luke 1:38) by her "Yes" to the angel Gabriel becomes the first earthly home for the one who will be our eternal home. Mary is addressed by the beautiful title "House of Gold" in the "Litany of Loreto," a prayer of praise and intercession stemming from the Middle Ages and given Church approval at the end of the sixteenth century. It is her wholehearted welcome of God into the humble home of her self that makes it possible for God to transform her into that "House of Gold." Mary's willingness to be a home for God to dwell in makes it possible for Jesus to become our true and lasting home.

Meditation: In what ways can you make your heart and your life an inviting home for God? Spend some time pondering one or two specific changes you are being invited to make.

Prayer: O Mary, House of Gold, help us prepare our hearts as welcoming homes for Jesus, Son of God and your son, so that he may be for us our eternal home. Amen.

December 19: Monday of the Fourth Week of Advent

Barrenness

O Antiphon:
O Root of Jesse's stem,
sign of God's love for all his people:
come to save us without delay!

Readings: Judg 13:2-7, 24-25a; Luke 1:5-25

Scripture:
In the days of Herod, King of Judea,
there was a priest named Zechariah
of the priestly division of Abijah;
his wife was from the daughters of Aaron,
and her name was Elizabeth.
Both were righteous in the eyes of God,
observing all the commandments
and ordinances of the Lord blamelessly.
But they had no child, because Elizabeth was barren
and both were advanced in years. (Luke 1:5-7)

Reflection: In the icy chill of late autumn and early winter
here in the north, we often look out over barren landscapes:
the stark, angular structure of leafless trees, dry dead grass
crumbling under foot, lifeless brown foliage clinging to oak
branches rattling like bones, the piercing chill of icy north
winds. These experiences quite naturally evoke our own

inner grief and desolation. Living in, or crossing, a bleak, lifeless desert brings up similar feelings. The landscape mirrors for us an inner emptiness, dryness, or chill that can haunt our days and nights even in the midst of a busy and seemingly productive life.

Many women in both the Hebrew and Christian Scriptures lamented their personal barrenness.

We all have relatives or friends, couples with whom we grieve because they long to conceive and bear children but cannot. And all of us, men and women, go through periods of barrenness in our lives: times when we are unable to conceive or give birth to ideas, images, new directions, changes of heart, healthy connections with other people. There are also times when, flat on our backs with sickness, we are unable to muster up the energy to care. With the barren women of the Bible we grieve, lament, and are tempted to despair. During seasons of our lives like these we long for warmth and light, for renewed energy and purpose.

The good news of today's liturgy is that out of our utmost desolation God can bring new life.

Meditation: What is old and worn out, dry, icy, without sap in your life? Allow it into your consciousness, entrust it to God, and pray for new life.

Prayer: God of new beginnings, you are the hope of the hopeless. Stir up in us anew the life of your Son Jesus, so that knowing the light and warmth of his Spirit we may share that light and warmth with others. Amen.

The Poor and Weak

O Antiphon:
O Key of David
opening the gates of God's eternal Kingdom:
come and free the prisoners of darkness!

Readings: Isa 7:10-14; Luke 1:26-38

Scripture:
And coming to [Mary], [the angel Gabriel] said,
"Hail, full of grace! The Lord is with you." (Luke 1:28)

Reflection: Mary "was greatly troubled" (Luke 1:29) when Gabriel addressed her as he did. Faithful Hebrew young woman that she was, no doubt she had a keen awareness of all the incidents like that recorded in the Hebrew Scriptures. Even though "The Lord is with you." (Luke 1:28b) was a common Hebrew greeting, when it came from an angel, a messenger of God, it had deeper significance, referring often to some challenging mission. Gabriel's words would have stirred up reminiscences that were deep in her soul.

Even before Mary had time to think much about the greeting, she would intuitively have known that what was going to be asked of her was no small thing, and as she "pondered what sort of greeting this might be" (Luke 1:29), her certainty about that—and perhaps her dread—increased.

When she heard that she was to mother the "Son of the Most High" who would "rule over the house of Jacob forever" on "the throne of David" (Luke 1:32-33), she must have been awestruck, and she responded by acknowledging her absolute inability as a single woman to do this. As sincere Christians we want, like Mary, to do God's will, but we too have fears about what is or might be asked of us. We are aware that it may be beyond our power to respond.

God, however, has a long history of approaching the poor and weak to be special instruments in carrying out the divine work in our world.

The same God who strengthened Israel and Mary in their fears—making their cooperation possible—will make possible for us whatever is necessary to carry out God's will.

Meditation: What beyond your power to give are you afraid God may be asking of you? Imagine Mary at your side and the angel Gabriel comforting you as he does her with the words: "Do not be afraid . . . the holy Spirit will come upon you, and the power of the Most High will overshadow you" (Luke 1:30b, 35a).

Prayer: God of all strength, please surround me with your messengers of courage as I face the challenges before me. Free me from my fears and renew my trust in you so that I may live in harmony with your will. Amen.

December 21: Wednesday of the Fourth Week of Advent

Come

O Antiphon:
O Radiant Dawn,
splendor of eternal light, sun of justice:
come and shine on those who dwell in darkness and in the
  shadow of death.

Readings: Song 2:8-14 or Zeph 3:14-18a; Luke 1:39-45

Scripture:
Hark! my lover—here he comes
  springing across the mountains,
  leaping across the hills. (Song 2:8)

Reflection: God, the lover, leaping toward us with wild delight speaks the fullness of that divine longing for us in one
word, "Come!" Our hearts awake to the irrepressible joy of
anticipation as we cry out "Let me see you, / let me hear
your voice," you who are hiding "in the clefts of the rock, /
in the secret recesses of the cliff" (Song 2:14b, 14a). "[Y]our
voice is sweet, / and you are lovely" (Song 2:14c). And our
response echoes the invitation of our divine lover, "Come!"

  Advent is all about deep longing for the *coming* of our
Divine Lover. The word Advent itself is taken from the
Latin verb *advenire* which means "to come to or toward."
Advent celebrates the wonderful reality that God who is

Love (see 1 John 4:8) is coming and will come to us. The divine desire for us echoes in our hearts as our desire for God and we cry, "Come!" During Advent we sing this love song over and over, "Come, Lord Jesus, do not delay."

When Jesus arrives at Elizabeth's house in the womb of his mother Mary, John the Baptist leaps for joy in his mother's womb. He dances for all of us who are jubilant at Jesus' coming in history, who are delighted by his veiled coming to us in daily life, and who anticipate with hope-filled eagerness his coming to us in death.

In the very last lines of the New Testament, in the Book of Revelation that looks forward to Christ's final coming in glory, this love song reaches its zenith in the full chorus of the Church: "The Spirit and the bride say, 'Come'" (Rev 22:17). And Jesus responds, "Yes, I am coming soon" (Rev 22:20). To which the author and all of us cry out with longing, "Amen! Come, Lord Jesus!" (Rev 22:20).

Meditation: Take some time to open and welcome your heart's deepest longing. Repeat slowly, "Come, Lord Jesus, do not delay." Let the words sink into ever more interior levels of your soul.

Prayer: Divine Lover of humanity, come and be with us now in our heart's deepest longings. Open us to the interior embrace of your love in the Spirit of Christ Jesus. Amen.

Exultation in God's Greatness

O Antiphon:
O King of all nations and keystone of the Church:
come and save [us], whom you formed from the dust!

Readings: 1 Sam 1:24-28; Luke 1:46-56

Scripture:
Mary said:

> "My soul proclaims the greatness of the Lord;
>   my spirit rejoices in God my savior,
>   for he has looked upon his lowly servant."

(Luke 1:46-48a)

Reflection: In today's gospel reading Mary proclaims God's greatness as the "Mighty One" whose mercy will be shown through her (see Luke 1:46-56) in her son Jesus. This proclamation mirrors Hannah's song of exultation in God in the responsorial psalm as she exults in the gift of her son Samuel (see 1 Sam 2).

Hannah's story is touching. She was the childless wife of Elkanah. Elkanah would say to her, "Hannah, why do you weep, and why do you refuse to eat? Why do you grieve? Am I not more to you than ten sons?" (1 Sam 1:8). Like Hannah we can feel bereft at some of life's deeply distress-

beloved Son; with you I am well pleased" (Mark 1:11)—the full manifestation that in Jesus, God is fully united with humanity.

Most of us have trouble sometime or another in life accepting our humanity. We chafe under its restrictions: sickness; fear; disappointments in love; limitations of intelligence, wealth, previous commitment, death. And we stagger under human possibilities: ecstatic joy, self-giving love, abiding peace. But Jesus says, "I choose everything about it. I love it. I want to be human." Rather than being any barrier to God, humanity in Jesus was shown to be God's preferred dwelling place and the matrix of divine saving power in our world (see Phil 2 and John 1).

Meditation: What limitations of yours seem to you to make it impossible for you to be God's abiding place? What possibilities for your life seem to be too wonderful to expect?

Prayer: Jesus, God's beloved Son and our brother, our baptism has made us participants in your divine life. In all our experiences of limitation and possibility open us to the transforming love of our relationship with God in you. Amen.

Embracing Humanity

Readings: Isa 42:1-4, 6-7; Acts 10:34-38; Mark 1:7-11

Scripture:
It happened in those days that Jesus . . .
 . . . was baptized in the Jordan by John. (Mark 1:9)

Reflection: What would prompt Jesus to seek out baptism from John? He was in no need of ritual or moral purification. In Matthew's Gospel Jesus tells John to allow his baptism since "it is fitting for us to fulfill all righteousness" (Matt 3:15b). In Scripture the word "righteousness" is used very often and has many meanings and connotations, some of them moral and legal, but others having to do with God's saving action in the world. Jesus is talking about the latter.

Descending into the waters of the Jordan is Jesus' way of walking fully and deliberately into his humanity. His actions proclaim: "I am human, just like you. Whatever is human I embrace with love. I lovingly embrace human limitations: experiences of weakness, fatigue, discouragement, fear, suffering, and death. And I lovingly embrace all human possibilities: human opportunities for enjoyment, creativity, and love reaching out into infinity." As Jesus completes the symbolic action of that acceptance walking up out of the water, the heavens are opened, the Spirit of God descends on him, and a voice declares, "You are my hear the somber, awe-struck kings break into rich three-part harmony as they carefully place their lavish gifts of gold, frankincense, and myrrh at the feet of this golden child, their camels and dromedaries (the one-humped variety!), halters shimmering, stretching their necks and legs in the background. Artists keep trying to capture some of the blinding glory of this divine manifestation. No matter that the gospel, as you may have noticed, never talks about three kings. Matthew identifies the visitors as magi, that is, wise men from the east, members of a hereditary priestly class from the land of the Medes and Persians!

The picture breaks through boundaries of geography, religion, and social status. The glory of God shines for all. The poor child Jesus is an infinitely rich and golden gift for people of every nation, race, religion, for those from the East and West, North and South.

Meditation: Look around your personal-spiritual horizon to reconnect with the star leading you on your journey to God made manifest in Jesus. Decide what next steps you need to take in order to bring the gift of yourself to him.

Prayer: Golden child, you who welcomed the magi with their gifts of gold, frankincense, and myrrh, receive the gift of ourselves and of the nations of the world that we offer to you today. Keep guiding us by the light of your star so that together we may reach our journey's destination with you in glory. Amen.

ing losses and failures—our experience of being "childless"—whatever that means for us: literally without a child, or without a job, without ideas, without a spouse, without a friend. A deep sense of inadequacy comes over us as we think we just do not, and will not ever, have whatever it is we need to be fulfilled. Looking around it seems like "other people" have had so much more success, are doing so much better, and are so much happier! These feelings can be especially keen when we think our inadequacy is disappointing to someone who loves us, even though that person may constantly reassure us about their appreciation and esteem for us. We, like Hannah, may be inconsolable, unable to realize how deeply we are loved. God is always with us saying, "Are you not more to me than many children, many ideas, many jobs, many friends. My love for you does not depend on anything you do or produce in life!"

Divine fruitfulness in us may not come in the way we had hoped for; it will, nevertheless, be the source of great exultation in God's greatness manifest in mercy and goodness to us.

Meditation: In what ways has the Divine Mercy been fruitful in your lowliness?

Prayer: Merciful God, the power of your greatness cannot be hindered by our weaknesses and inadequacies. Look upon us kindly and bring to birth in our lives whatever will be for our good and your glory. This we pray through your Son, Jesus who lives in us. Amen.

December 23: Friday of the Fourth Week of Advent

Fire and Lye

O Antiphon:
O Emmanuel, our King and Giver of Law:
come to save us, Lord our God!

Readings: Mal 3:1-4, 23-24; Luke 1:57-66

Scripture:
But who will endure the day of his coming?
    And who can stand when he appears?
For he is like the refiner's fire,
    or like the fuller's lye. (Mal 3:2)

Reflection: If this reading does not stop us up short and raise some fear and trepidation in our hearts, we probably haven't really heard it! To celebrate Christmas as God's coming among us as a helpless child is one thing. But coming face-to-face with the overpowering splendor of God in Christ now, at the time of our death, or in his final coming in glory is an awesome prospect. God is loving, but the love of God is a fiery furnace. God is merciful, but the mercy of God is the strongest bleach that exists. Picture the most beautiful silver or gold piece you have ever seen. What a thing of joy it is! But it only got that way through fire! Imagine a shining, bright fabric that catches your eye and stirs your heart. How you love to look at it. Only its bath in bleach made it so. The fire and lye of God's presence is not for our destruction but for our transformation. God wants to make us into that beautiful vessel, that exquisite cloth.

Like the Hebrew community of Malachi's time, our receptivity to God's love is skewed by our narrow self-interest, our need to protect and control our lives so we can have and keep what we think we need to be happy—the fear-based prejudice and greed that keeps us individually and as a national and international community from living justly. But God's love will not let us be less than we are called to be.

Meditation: What prejudice, greed, narrow self-interest or exaggerated need to protect or control may be a barrier to God's work in you? Pray for the willingness to allow God to purify you of these.

Prayer: God of fire and lye, without your purifying work in us through the dying and rising of Jesus your Son, we will not be able to know your love and see your glory. Cleanse and refine our spirits in whatever ways you know we can take so that we can be worthy vessels of your glory. Amen.

Dawn from on High

Readings: 2 Sam 7:1-5, 8b-12, 14a, 16; Luke 1:67-79

Scripture:
"In the tender compassion of our God
   the dawn from on high shall break upon us,
   to shine on those who dwell in darkness and the
      shadow of death,
   and to guide our feet into the way of peace." (Luke 1:78-79)

Reflection: The symbolic interplay between the light of the sun and the divine light in Christ evokes a deep response in the Christian soul. This year the winter solstice in the northern hemisphere was on December 21st at 12:35 p.m. (CST). It was then that the sun reached the southernmost point of its journey giving us in the north our longest night and shortest day. It was at that moment also that "the sun reversed its course" and daylight hours began to increase little by little as the sun took up its journey back north. December 25th was not identified as the date of Christ's birth until the third century C.E. The reasons for that choice are not completely clear, but after it was accepted, Christian writers began to connect the human birth of the Son of God with a popular holiday in the Roman empire that celebrated the winter solstice as the return of increasing sunlight.

The O Antiphon sung on the day of the winter solstice was "O Radiant Dawn, / splendor of eternal light, sun of justice: / come and shine on those who dwell in darkness and in the shadow of death!"

Advent is the darkest time of our year in the northern hemisphere. That physical darkness resonates with our interior nights. Sometimes these are comforting experiences of darkness in which a hidden light reveals itself to us if we wait—nights as the psalmist says, that are shining as the day (see Ps 139:12). Other times these nights oppress us with the opaque darkness of sin and death. In both kinds of darkness we are invited to stay alert and receptive to the coming light of Christ. Whether or not the connection between the physical lengthening of sunlight and the dawn of the Light of the Son was the original motivation for settling on December 25th as the date for Christmas, the hope engendered by increasing daylight resonates with the hope of the individual and of the world who dwelling "in darkness and death's shadow" (Luke 1:79) wait for "the daybreak from on high" to "visit us" (Luke 1:78).

Meditation: Sitting in the dark (or semi-dark) call to mind some experience of physical, psychological, or spiritual darkness. Slowly and trustingly repeat the words: "The dawn from on high shall break upon us" (Luke 1:78, *Lectionary*).

Prayer: "O Radiant Dawn, / splendor of eternal light, sun of justice: / come and shine on [us] who dwell in darkness and in the shadow of death!" Amen.

CHRISTMAS AND DAYS
WITHIN ITS OCTAVE

December 25: Solemnity of Christmas

Vigil Mass: Hope

Readings: Isa 62:1-5; Acts 13:16-17, 22-25; Matt 1:1-25 or 1:18-25

Scripture:
You shall be a glorious crown in the hand of the LORD,
  a royal diadem held by your God.
No more shall people call you "Forsaken,"
  or your land "Desolate,"
but you shall be called "My Delight,"
  and your land "Espoused." (Isa 62:3-4ab)

Reflection: The eager joy and longing of Advent today reach their zenith. The four-week watch we have been keeping—in growing darkness in the northern hemisphere and in the growing light of the southern hemisphere—peak in the final day of our waiting for the Christmas festival, the liturgical celebration of God's coming in Jesus' birth at Bethlehem.

Many of us have fond childhood memories of the day before Christmas. We may recall the magical atmosphere set for us as toddlers and young children as someone read to us that traditional children's poem, "'Twas the Night Before Christmas." A sense of hope-filled and excited expectation were irrepressible as we tried to settle down that afternoon and evening and look forward to Christmas morning. Finally we had come to the "last sleep" before the big celebration, and we knew something good was coming: a family celebration, perhaps toys from Santa Claus, Saint Nick, or the Christ Child, depending on our family customs. We went to sleep reluctantly, so keyed up were we by those happy thoughts. For some of us, because of our poverty, there were few, if any, gifts, but lots of love. The scarcity of gifts may have included emotional deprivation or abuse so that there was nothing for us but sadness about the coming day. Even if there would be expensive gifts, we would not have what we really needed: warmth and affection.

No matter what our childhood experience and its lasting effects, the hope engendered by this day in the liturgical year is not unfounded and will ultimately never disappoint us. God's desire not just to give us gifts but to be *The Gift* for and in our humanity is shouted out by Isaiah: "As a young man marries a virgin, / your Builder shall marry you" (Isa 62:5). Our longing to rise up singing and shouting about this incomprehensible wonder of God's goodness (see Ps 89:2) coming to us in Jesus can hardly be contained. Standing through the reading of the long version of the gospel, Matthew's genealogy, recapitulates for us the long historical human waiting through darkness and light for the long-hoped-for coming of the Messiah. Joseph's willingness to accept in faith the angel's word about the divine origin of this child in spite of the confusion about Mary's pregnancy encourages our belief in God's goodness even in the midst of darkness and doubt. Divine Love cannot rest until it becomes God's enfleshed covenant with us in Jesus in whom heaven is wedded to earth. Like a spouse delighting in the union with his beloved, God delights in this union of the Divinity with humanity (see Isa 62:5), and our anticipation of the wedding celebration fills us with joy about to burst.

Meditation: Get in touch with your deepest desire and any weariness or discouragement that dulls your hope in its fulfillment. In faith entrust both to God.

Prayer: God of hope, in expectant darkness we wait for the gift of your salvation. We pray with confidence trusting that you will not fail to bring new light into our lives and world through your Son Jesus. Amen.

Mass at Midnight: Good News for the Poor

Readings: Isa 9:1-6; Titus 2:11-14; Luke 2:1-14

Scripture:
While they were there,
  the time came for her to have her child,
  and she gave birth to he firstborn son.
She wrapped him in swaddling clothes and laid him in a
      manger,
  because there was no room for them in the inn.
    (Luke 2:6-7)

Reflection: The joy of Christmas is for everyone; it is a time for all of us to be glad because the one who was born on this day is Life itself, our hope for and way into eternal life. When God becomes human in Jesus our humanity is fully embraced by the divine, and nobody is excluded.

Midnight Mass, however, seems to highlight especially God's identification with the poor, the weak, the outcast, the marginal. God comes as a helpless child born in an animal shelter of poor parents who could find no guest room in Bethlehem, overcrowded as it was because of the census. And in Luke's narrative the first news of God's identification with us does not go to the wealthy or those in high political or religious positions but to some poor shepherds, people who were without wealth, power, or privilege. How mysterious! How strange and wonderful! God to whom all riches belong wants to become poor like us and to be sure that the poor and lowly are the first to hear about it.

Used to being left alone during their long, dark nights in the fields where they watched over their flocks, the shepherds were terrified at the appearance of the angelic messenger surrounded by the glory of God. Imagine some of us who clean office buildings at night, or who work the night shifts in factories, bakeries, hospitals, restaurant kitchens, or as security guards in dark parking lots. Or think of poor parents watching through the night with sick children. Picture how it would be for them to be suddenly surrounded by the brilliant light of God's glory surpassing many times over the strength of any light by which they work or watch. What a breathtaking shock! Of course, we are all poor in a radical way. Nothing we "have" really belongs to us; nothing we are is anything we have not been given. Our very being is absolutely dependent on our divine source. We would all have reason to be awestruck by such an extraordinary manifestation of God's greatness, God's glory, an infinite contrast to our poverty.

This night in 2005 is still the night of the shepherds. Seen or unseen, noticed or unnoticed, in faith we know that the light that surrounded them surrounds us. The angel who proclaimed the good news to them is proclaiming the good news to us. The same God who had come into their world as a helpless infant in the manger uniting divinity to their humanity and identifying with them in their poverty, that same God in Jesus continues to live in our world identified with us in our lowliness and poverty, one with us in our humanity. The angel's message to the shepherds is also for us: "Do not be afraid; for behold, I proclaim to you good news of great joy that will be for all the people. For today in the city of David a savior has been born for you who is Messiah and Lord" (Luke 2:10-11).

Meditation: Imagine the poor people in your neighborhood, city, or country to whom God wishes to proclaim "good news of great joy" (Luke 2:10b). Open your heart to them in prayer. And be alert to ways you could help bring that good news to them.

Prayer: God of glory and might, tonight we celebrate your coming into our world as a poor and lowly child born of parents away from home and without adequate shelter. Give strength and sustenance especially to homeless and poverty-stricken children and their parents. May your glory and might manifested through the generosity of others fill them with the joy of your presence in Jesus our brother. Amen.

Mass at Dawn: Kindness

Readings: Isa 62:11-12; Titus 3:4-7; Luke 2:15-20

Scripture:
When the kindness and generous love
    of God our savior appeared,
not because of any righteous deeds we had done
    but because of his mercy,
he saved us through the bath of rebirth
    and renewal by the Holy Spirit. (Titus 3:4-5)

Reflection: In the early Christmas morning, as the first rays of light herald the sun's rising in the eastern sky, our hearts open to the dawn of a new reality that entered human life at Jesus' birth, and which rises in our own hearts each morning. With Mary we are still pondering the full meaning of that light. What does God's becoming one of us in Jesus mean in our lives? Paul's words to Titus in the second reading give us some insight. In Jesus, he says, "the kindness and generous love / of God our savior appeared," and this kindness and love God pours out on us in the Holy Spirit through baptism, the "bath of rebirth" (Titus 3:4, 5b).

The fullness of God's kindness and generous love in Jesus' lifetime on earth is made known only one day, one moment, one year at a time through his words and actions that culminate in the triumph of love poured out in his suffering, death, and resurrection. Our baptismal experience of God's love and kindness in Christ, permeating our lives, is also made known only through the course of a lifetime that inevitably includes darkness, suffering, and death.

In an interview published in *The Way of Woman: Awakening the Perennial Feminine* (New York: Doubleday, 1995), Helen Luke quotes a letter of C. J. Jung who said, "There is a mystical fool in me who goes beyond all science." She continues, "And he went on to say that because of this he had suffered deeply and had known great darkness. But always in the midst of the darkness there was a shining light." And he ends by saying, "Somewhere there seems to be great kindness in the abysmal darkness of the Deity" (p. 183).

Though Jung was not connecting this light with Jesus, from the standpoint of our Christmas faith experience Christ is that light that shines somewhere in the midst of even our darkest moments. And what is that light, that "great kindness" that dawns daily in our lives, doing for us? The word "kindness," Helen Luke goes on to explain, has the deep meaning of "kinship with every person, every animal, every plant—the entire creation. Everything is kin" (ibid., 183–84). Moment by moment, day by day, the never-failing kindly Light shining in our darkness remains present and at work uniting us all in kindness, in kinship.

Meditation: In what heart-expanding ways have you experienced the kindness of God in your life even in the midst of suffering?

Prayer: Infinite Kindness united to us in Jesus, enlarge the narrow passageways of our hearts filling them with your love and compassion. With that gift from you may we do our part in bringing about the kinship you desire for the human family. Amen.

Mass During the Day: Word of God

Readings: Isa 52:7-10; Heb 1:1-6; John 1:1-18 or 1:1-5, 9-14

Scripture:
And the Word became flesh
   and made his dwelling among us,
   and we saw the glory,
   the glory as of the Father's only Son
   full of grace and truth. (John 1:14)

Reflection: Words, words, words! My office is filled with words: books full of them, newsletters overflowing with them, files (that have collected thousands of my own words and tens of thousands of others), compact disks electronically coded with words, a computer hard drive safeguarding millions of them and with links to a network where I can be in touch with zillions of other words, a radio I can turn on anytime and hook up with words flying around the atmosphere on multiple waves. What is it that keeps us talking and listening, reading and writing?

Human communication is complex. Research on its various dynamics is never ending. Learning to engage in it positively is a lifetime challenge. During our waking hours we spend much of our time working to find words that help us get in touch and give expression and shape to our ideas, our feelings, our selves, and learning to listen to others so that we can make connections and develop our relationships. Communicating with each other—sharing our ideas, our insights, our feelings, and our perspectives—and listening to others, and finally learning to commune in peace at a level beyond words, are a big part of what it means to be human. Perhaps most deeply we are striving with our words to give our selves, and in our listening we are striving to receive others.

God's Word is God's gift of God's self to us; our silent attentive listening with our physical ears and with the inner ear of faith is our welcome of that Word. In the past, as the author of Hebrews tells us, "God spoke in partial and various ways to our ancestors through the prophets." But now, "in these last days, he spoke to us through a son" (Heb 1:1-2). The Son, the Word of God was "In the beginning" not only "with God," but "was God" (John 1:1). It was through the Son that God created the world (John 1:3). He is the One who shares the full light of divine glory, and is the "very imprint of [God's] being" (Heb 1:3). Now John tells us this Divine Word has come in our human flesh to live with us, not only to stand beside us, to be our neighbor, our friend, but even more than that, the Son of God, the Divine Word has come to make us God's children, sharers in the Divine Life (see John 1:12-13). As we listen in silent faith with our inner ear to the Word of God made flesh, we are drawn into God's inner life. Our silent welcome of the Word of God in Jesus allows him to be the Life of our life, the Love of our love, the Light of our light.

Meditation: Take fifteen or twenty minutes of time apart in a quiet place. After you settle in, begin repeating slowly first in a low voice, then with your lips only, and finally merely in interior imagination: "Word of God made flesh, come let us adore." Let the words become more and more interior and then drop away until only one word is repeating itself deep within your being. Let that disappear and sit in stillness.

Prayer: Welcome, Word of God made flesh. As we hear you in the words of Scripture and in your Word inscribed in our own flesh, may our outer and inner voices fall silent so that we may worship you in quiet awe. Amen.

Witnesses

Readings: Acts 6:8-10; 7:54-59; Matt 10:17-22

Scripture:
When they heard [what Stephen said], they were infuriated,
   and they ground their teeth at him. (Acts 7:54)

Reflection: Celebrating the feast of the first martyr comes
as a shock on the day after Christmas. The readings of this
day bring us face-to-face with divisions that surface because of the personal entrance of Divine Love in Jesus into
our world. The joy, the comforting love, the gift giving, the
longed for peace of Christmas seem suddenly far off as we
picture the "infuriated" enemies of Stephen who "ground
their teeth at him" as "filled with the holy Spirit" (Acts
7:54) he proclaims his vision of "the glory of God and Jesus
standing at the right hand of God" (Acts 7:55). The gospel
reading warns us that, like Stephen, as witnesses to Christ
we need to be ready for opposition and persecution. In con-
sidering challenges that we, like Stephen, face, we have
something to learn not only from him but more surpris-
ingly also from his persecutors.

Willingness to expand our religious understanding is not
easy for us either. New ways of interpreting religious reality
can stir up a great deal of insecurity and fear in us. Often
our first defense is refusal to listen, followed by attempts to

shout louder than any person offering a way of interpretation different from ours. Next come attempts to stop them from speaking altogether. Our desperate need to be "right" because of our fear can obscure the possibility of our expanding and deepening our understanding of the truth. In doing so we may consider ourselves to be like Stephen in witnessing to the faith, while in reality we may sometimes be more like his accusers and opponents.

Being witnesses to Christ doesn't mean we have all the answers about the meaning of Jesus' life, death, and resurrection. When we are challenged to be witnesses, we need to listen to others, to let go of worry about our arguments, and trust that the Spirit at work in us will help us to promote God's reign of love.

Meditation: In what ways am I being invited to expand my religious understanding and imagination? Are there ways I have been stopping up my ears, out-shouting my potential dialogue partners, and cutting them out of my life?

Prayer: Jesus, through your birth, life, death, and resurrection you give witness to a loving God who is more than our minds can ever comprehend. Stephen stood firm in his witness to you and your challenging message. Through his intercession may we grow in our ability to listen deeply for your truth wherever we hear it, and to speak of it to others with humility, respect, peace, and confidence. Amen.

December 27: Feast of St. John, Apostle and Evangelist

Friends

Readings: 1 John 1:1-4; John 20:1a, 2-8

Scripture:
On the first day of the week,
    Mary Magdalene . . . ran and went to Simon Peter
    and to the other disciple whom Jesus loved, and told
      them,
    "They have taken the Lord from the tomb,
    and we do not know where they put him." (John 20:1a, 2)

Reflection: Jesus had friends whom he cared about very much and to whom he related in great intimacy. Three of Jesus' closest friends are part of today's gospel scene: Mary Magdalene, Simon Peter, and John the Evangelist, whose feast we are celebrating. With these friends Jesus shared his deepest thoughts and feelings, and they in turn entered into the same kind of trusting, open, loving relationship with him.

On this feast day, sharing in a cup of "St. John's love," that is, a glass of blessed wine, has been a treasured custom in some Christian communities and families. The wine, which so readily brings to mind for us the eucharistic wine, is a symbol of the rich, healing love of Christ that filled the heart of John and today fills our hearts.

John's reference to himself several times in his gospel, as in today's passage, as the "disciple whom Jesus loved" (John 20:2), reveals his certainty about how close Jesus was to him and how he treasured and savored this special relationship. Like Mary Magdalene he had stayed with Jesus through the terrible ordeal of his death by crucifixion (see John 19:26).

Jesus identifies not only John and the other disciples who are present but all of us as recipients of his intimate love when he says in his final discourse: "I no longer call you slaves, because a slave does not know what his master is doing. I have called you friends, because I have told you everything I have heard from my Father" (John 15:15). So today we all drink in gratitude the "love of St. John," that is, we refresh and renew our spirits by receiving in joy the superabundant drink of God's loving Spirit, the intimate love of God that Jesus shares with John and us, his friends.

Meditation: Note some of the ways you have enjoyed friendship with God. Recall also with gratitude some particular friends who have enriched your life in ways that have made you more yourself and brought you closer to God.

Prayer: Friend of every human soul, expand our hearts with your love in the Spirit of Jesus so that we may know how to live in love with you and grow in faithful friendship with the companions you give us to share life in our time and place. Amen.

Herod

Readings: 1 John 1:5–2:2; Matt 2:13-18

Scripture:
When Herod realized that he had been deceived by the magi, he became furious. (Matt 2:16a)

Reflection: The cruel murder of the Holy Innocents that marks this day of the liturgical year is again, like the martyrdom of Stephen, a shocking contrast to the joy and peace of Christmas. Outside of this account in the Gospel of Matthew, there is no historical reference to the slaughter of "all the boys" "two years old and under in Bethlehem and its vicinity" (Matt 2:16b), but this turn of events would not be inconsistent with what is known about Herod. Though he accomplished many good things for Palestine through his political connections, these were often the result of power brokering.

How could anyone be so worried about their power and prestige that they would murder innocent children, or for that matter, adults? Today many of the children who die violent deaths are killed by a parent or caregiver, someone on whom they are absolutely dependent, and many other innocent victims die because of the neglect or aggression of governing powers and military forces whose duty it is to protect and promote human life. Why do we keep doing this? Who will free us from this trap?

"Herod" is still alive in unjust social, political, and economic systems. He gets his power from the multiplied and strengthened hatred and jealousy of each "Herod" who lives in us individually.

"Rachel" also lives in us, weeping for the abused, the oppressed, the neglected, the murdered—especially innocent children. And there is in each of us a loving mother and father who would, like Mary and Joseph, flee to safety with them. Most importantly *Christ lives within us.* His divine love is in our world in Jesus who freely pours out in us God's infinite and unconditional love. God alone, present within us in Christ, our only deep and lasting security, can free us from "Herod."

Meditation: Tune in to the "Herod-Rachel" drama going on within you and in our world. What new and creative expressions of life is "Herod" snuffing out? Can you hear "Rachel" grieving? Call on the Christ to console "Rachel" and to free poor "Herod" from the need to dominate.

Prayer: Source of peace and reconciliation, free us from violent thoughts, feelings, and actions, and forgive us for the suffering these have caused ourselves and others around us. May your grace touching us through these suffering innocents and through the weeping of their parents open our hearts fully to your Son Jesus so that in him we may bring your healing to our world. Amen.

December 29: The Fifth Day in the Octave of Christmas

The Light of Love

Readings: 1 John 2:3-11; Luke 2:22-35

Scripture:
[T]he darkness is passing away,
and the true light is already shining. (1 John 2:8b)

Reflection: Sunshine makes a great deal of difference in our lives. Without it life on earth would not be possible—at least not life as we know it. We need light for our physical and emotional well-being. In recent years more and more research has been done on SAD, seasonal affective disorder, which is depression experienced by quite a number of people because of decreasing amounts of daylight in the fall and winter months of the northern hemisphere. Maybe that is what attracts us to celebrating Christmas with lots of lights: Christmas tree lights, luminaria (those lovely glowing candles set in paper bags along sidewalks and roads leading to homes), the warm and inviting light of fireplaces and potbellied stoves. Living in darkness intensifies our longing for the light.

The experience of spiritual darkness increases our desire for spiritual light. Just as we cannot flourish without physical light, so we cannot thrive without spiritual light. That spiritual light, John tells us in today's first reading, is connected with love, while spiritual darkness is a companion of hatred.

Sometimes it seems like our world is caught up in a kind of spiritual "SADness," a depressed state coming from a scarcity of the light of love. Experiences of hatred that someone or some group directs at you, or your own hatred toward someone or some group—both are difficult to bear. All of us are both givers and receivers of hatred. If others have somehow injured us, or if we feel treated unjustly, we are tempted to stay hardened in a stance of deep hostility toward them. Or we hate others (or others hate us) for no particular reason except they (or we) are who they (or we) are.

In Jesus, John tells us, "the darkness is passing away, and the true light is already shining" (1 John 2:8b). The light, God's love in Jesus, is accessible to us. When we are caught and feeling helpless in the darkness of hatred—ours toward others or theirs toward us—we can call on him to free us by the power of his Spirit.

Meditation: Sit in a patch of sunlight, firelight, or lamp-light and absorb its warmth and comfort. Do this as a way of intentionally opening to the divine light of love.

Prayer: Sun of our lives, true light of our hearts, you have come into our world through the birth of your Son Jesus. Open our eyes to your light, free us from sadness and hatred so that we may rejoice with one another in that birth now and come to live with you in Jesus forever. Amen.

December 30: Feast of the Holy Family
(Roman Catholic Church)

The Sixth Day in the Octave of Christmas
(Episcopal Church)

Aunts and Uncles

Readings: Gen 15:1-6; 21:1-3; Heb 11:8, 11-12, 17-19;
Luke 2:22-40; alternatively: Sir 3:2-6, 12-14; Col 3:12-21 or
3:12-17, Matt 2:13-15, 19-23a

Scripture:
[The parents of Jesus] took him up to Jerusalem
to present him to the Lord. (Luke 2:22b)

Reflection: Family religious and cultural celebrations connect us with our roots and give us a sense of our identity. In
many families single, lonely neighbors are included. You
may recall "Aunt Sadie" or "Uncle Ben" coming for Thanks-
giving or Christmas dinner, and finding out only years
later that they were really no aunt or uncle of yours at all,
but elderly single people with no nearby relatives whom
your mother had befriended!

Mary and Joseph made sure that their family celebrated
the traditional religious and cultural rituals. Two of these
are the subject of today's gospel. The first is the purification
of a new mother (see Lev 12:1-8), a custom based on the no-
tion that ritual impurity was the result of giving birth, an
idea foreign to our way of thinking. The second is the con-

secration of the firstborn to God (see Exod 13:1-2, 11-16). Simeon and Anna, who appear in the passage immediately following today's gospel reading, were an integral part of the action during these festivities.

We can imagine Mary and Joseph feeling some anxiety when they came to the temple. They trusted God but surely must have wondered how this special son of theirs would develop. Because Simeon and Anna were so full of faith, so prayerful, so Spirit-filled, they were able to offer deep assurance about this child and his identity, as well as some honest forewarning about the suffering their parenthood would bring.

Maybe our "Aunt Sadies" and "Uncle Bens" are the "Annas" and "Simeons" of our lives. Filled with the Spirit they can amaze us with the insight and wisdom we need to understand our identity and mission. Or maybe you are that elderly aunt or that weathered uncle—one whose love and support are critical to the younger generation.

Meditation: Recall what you have learned from your aunts, uncles, elderly neighbors, and friends. What would you like to say to them?

Prayer: Wisdom of the ages, you touch our lives through the prophets and sages in our families and neighborhoods. Help us open our ears, minds, and hearts to the inspiration, comfort, direction, and strength that you provide in our lives through them. We ask this in the name of your son, Jesus. Amen.

Grace and Truth

Readings: 1 John 2:18-21; John 1:1-18

Scripture:
And the Word became flesh
and made his dwelling among us. (John 1:14a)

Reflection: The blazing glory of God taking as its tent a fragile human nature (just like ours!) presents such an enormous contrast that it seems almost preposterous. But that is precisely the startling truth of the incarnation revealed by John.

In the Exodus the Israelites experienced God's presence going ahead of them through the desert "in the daytime by means of a column of cloud to show them the way, and at night by means of a column of fire to give them light" (Exod 13:21). At Sinai God's awesome presence in fire wrapping the mountain in a cloud of smoke was so fierce that the people were warned not to try breaking through it lest they die (see Exod 19:16-25). As they continued on their way the Israelites recognized from afar this fiery divine presence, often called the *Shekinah* or "the Glory," especially hovering around the Tent of Meeting that sheltered the ark of the covenant. The literal meaning of the Greek word John uses in today's gospel reading for "made his dwelling" (John 1:14a, *Lectionary*) is "pitched his tent." In

Jesus, God's awe-inspiring glory is sheltered, interiorized, and made approachable in a tent of flesh so that we can experience God's grace and truth face-to-face.

Gracious and graceful people and things, and those that are true and genuine, naturally attract us, evoking joy, praise, and gratitude. Gracious neighbors, graceful dance partners, genuine crystal, real diamonds, true friends touch our hearts as well as our minds. The "grace and truth" (John 1:14e) that fill the glory of God in Jesus are not abstractions beyond our experience but the delightful presence of God embodied in our humanity in a way that stirs our affection. The Word of God made flesh in Jesus invites our personal love. The Word's fidelity lives in every genuine person and thing and surpasses them in length, depth, height, and strength (see Eph 4:18). The Word's graciousness and beauty shine in and beyond the splendor of nature, art, and our loveliest neighbors.

Meditation: Through your mind's eye gaze on some of the loveliest things and most gracious people you know. Consciously connect their goodness and its radiance in your life with the grace and truth of God in Jesus Christ. Spend some time praising God for this.

Prayer: Source of all truth and grace, your radiant goodness lives among us in Jesus your Son. Remove our blindness so that we may grow in appreciation of his radiant presence among us. Amen.

SOLEMNITY OF MARY TO
THE BAPTISM OF THE LORD

January 1: Solemnity of Mary, Mother of God
(Roman Catholic Church)

The Holy Name (Episcopal Church)

Reading

Readings: Num 6:22-27; Gal 4:4-7; Luke 2:16-21

Scripture:
And Mary kept all these things,
reflecting on them in her heart (Luke 2:19).

Reflection: In many traditional art images of Mary, especially those of the Annunciation, she is pictured with an open book. Mary's receptivity to the Word of God in Holy Scripture made her receptive to that Word in life. It takes courage to be an open-minded, open-hearted reader. It takes courage to be receptive to what is beyond the scope of our experience and imagination.

Today when the shepherds arrive with their message, Mary continues to read the book of God's Word, the book of life. She takes in the wonder-filled communication about her child. The receptivity she manifested when the angel Gabriel announced the unimaginable mystery of God's taking on humanity in her womb continues to deepen. Though fearful then, she had not stopped up her ears, nor closed her heart or mind.

Mary reads, mulls, integrates the Word of God so totally in her being that she becomes the book inscribed with the Word of God for us. Mary the book, Jesus the Word. Reading Mary, opening our whole being with her to Jesus, the Word of God inscribed in her life, we can become like her: courageous and welcoming of the Divine will in our lives, transformed like her by that Word taking over more and more in the flesh of our lives.

Meditation: In what ways could you keep the book of Mary open before you—pondering its contents, integrating its message with your life? Can you "read yourself" in Mary?: Mary asked to say "Yes" to God's will in a way she does not fully understand; Mary the single mother alienated from her fiancé; Mary proclaiming God's greatness and the triumph of the lowly; Mary giving birth far from home in an animal shelter; Mary fleeing to save her child from murder; Mary watching her child grow; Mary on pilgrimage losing her son; Mary realizing her son's countercultural mission; Mary sharing the life of Jesus' disciples; Mary whose prophetic son is hunted down by the authorities; Mary watching the cruel execution of her innocent son; Mary among the fearful apostles realizing the risen presence of her son in the coming of the Spirit.

Prayer: Word of God inscribed in the book of Mary, through her intercession teach us to read courageously, ponder deeply, and consent whole-heartedly to our transformation by your Spirit. Amen.

Staying

Readings: 1 John 2:22-28; John 1:19-28

Scripture:
As for you,
    the anointing that you received from him remains in you,
    so that you do not need anyone to teach you.
        (1 John 2:27a)

Reflection: In Luke's Gospel is that poignant scene where
the two disciples trudging dejectedly back to Emmaus after
the crucifixion invite the stranger who had joined them to
"Stay with us, for it is almost evening and the day is almost
over" (Luke 24:29b). As it turns out the stranger was Jesus
himself. It was he who had restored their hope by illumi-
nating for them the meaning of his death in a way that
made their hearts burn within them. Of course they would
want him to stay with them. Wanting someone to stay with
us is most often, if not always, an expression of our love,
our appreciation, our need, our desire for that person's
presence—which has come to mean so much to us.

In John's Gospel and in his first letter, the one from which
we read today, Jesus' remaining with us and our remaining
with him is a major theme. The word "remain" is used six
times in this short passage. Because the anointing, that is
the Holy Spirit, is the Son's gift which "remains in [us]" we

are able and urged to "remain in him" (1 John 2:27). Staying with Jesus and having Jesus stay with us is more than having him near us, even next to us. It is living in him and his living in us. This is what the disciples going to Emmaus had begun to experience.

Life requires a lot of staying power—not that staying is a good idea when we are in a destructive place, and knowing what is destructive is not always easy. It takes some wise discernment! But there are times when life is tough and we know we have to stay: times of sickness, times of job insecurity, times of conflict, times of demanding work, challenging study, difficult decisions, confusing relationships. At times like these it is so good to remember that we are not alone. We have the staying power we need because we are abiding in Christ, and he is abiding in us: he is the vine and we are the branches (see John 15:5a). Our staying, remaining, abiding in Jesus and his staying, remaining, abiding in us is the source of all our staying power in life and through death.

Meditation: Entrust yourself to Christ abiding in you. Reflect on those areas of your life that currently require your staying power and invite Christ to stay with you as you face them.

Prayer: Christ the Vine, you are our source of life and strength without whom we can do nothing. Thank you for abiding in us so that together we may abide in you now and forever. Amen.

January 3

Seeing

Readings: 1 John 2:29–3:6; John 1:29-34

Scripture:
Beloved, we are God's children now;
  what we shall be has not yet been revealed.
We do know that when it is revealed we shall be like him,
  for we shall see him as he is. (1 John 3:2)

Reflection: God became human in Jesus so that we might share in Divinity, they said in the early church. In the Mass, during the preparation of gifts, the priest (privately) says a special prayer as he mixes a little water with the wine. (In the old Latin Mass this was said aloud.) In it he implores that by the mystery symbolized in this mingling, God, who had deigned to share our humanity in Christ, grant us in Christ participation in the Divinity. This belief that we are invited into transforming union with God in Christ can be traced from the earliest Christian writers down through the centuries. It was called *theosis*, that is, deification. The belief is based in Scripture passages such as the one we read from 1 John today.

Our transformation in Christ is a process of "opening our eyes to the deifying light" (St. Benedict's way of speaking in the Prologue to his *Rule*!) that God has joined to humanity in Christ. Seeing God as God is in that light will make us like God. For years this statement about becoming able to see God as God is—and in so doing becoming like God has fascinated me (see 1 John 3:2). I have wondered how it is possible if God is infinite. No finite mind can comprehend infinity as an object separate from itself.

But what if we think not of being "here" and looking at God as an object "over there" but rather realize that by our baptism we ourselves are standing in God sharing from the inside in the divine act of seeing. As our life of prayer and sacramental celebration deepen, we shift more and more into that perspective. We come to see from God's point of view, from within "the Eye" that is God, and so we see as God does. Now others are no longer objects over, against, or in opposition to ourselves, but we are one with all other human participants in that seeing. Becoming like God is a shift away from a separated self-consciousness toward a consciousness which, though it remains distinct, is a consciousness united with the Divine and with all others who participate in the divine consciousness in Christ.

Meditation: Gently close your eyes and let thoughts drop away. By simple, trusting intention open to the divine consciousness, the Eye of God, who looks out lovingly from within your spirit.

Prayer: God of our Savior Jesus Christ, you took on our humanity so that we may share your life. Increase our faith and trust in that reality so that we may see as you see, love as you love in Christ our brother. Amen.

January 4

Looking

Readings: 1 John 3:7-10; John 1:35-42

Scripture:
The two disciples heard what [John the Baptist] said and
     followed Jesus.
Jesus turned and saw them following him and said to them,
   "What are you looking for?"
They said to him, "Rabbi" (which translated means Teacher),
   "where are you staying?"
He said to them, "Come, and you will see."
So they went and saw where he was staying,
   and they stayed with him that day. (John 1:37-39b)

Reflection: "What are you looking for?" This is one of life's fundamental questions, perhaps its most important. Today Jesus is asking it of us. What is your honest response? What is it you really want? Can you let yourself be honest about that? You are being invited to say not what you think you should want, or what you think other people would want, or what others would want you to want! But, what are *you* looking for? Is it those things that were on your Christmas list? That wish you made before you blew out your birthday candles? The products, entertainment opportunities, self-improvement plans that dominate TV ads and pop up on your computer screen? Peace on earth? Peace in your family? Peace in your soul? Perhaps all of the above—and much more besides. But what is your deepest desire? Can you get in touch with that?

When the disciple's were asked, "What are you looking for?" they respond, "Rabbi . . . where are you staying?" (John 1:38). Why? Was it just an off the cuff response quickly given because they were taken by surprise? And even if it was, might it have been included in John's Gospel because it has some deeper meaning? What about where Jesus was staying would be important to them? Does it imply, "We think it might be you we are looking for, but we are not sure yet, so we'd like to be more certain about who you are, where your roots are, where you are at home." Or maybe it means, "We know it is you we are looking for; you are so attractive to us we do not want to lose contact with you; we want to know where we can find you. We want to be able to go and be with you in the place where you are at home."

Meditation: What are you looking for? Does it have anything to do with where Jesus is staying?

Prayer: Jesus, Teacher and Guide, give us the grace to be honest about what we are looking for, and to learn, as we are able with your help, to look for you in and beyond all other desires. Amen.

January 5

Loving in Deed and Truth

Readings: 1 John 3:11-21; John 1:43-51

Scripture:
If someone who has worldly means
  sees a brother in need and refuses him compassion,
  how can the love of God remain in him?
Children, let us love not in word or speech
  but in deed and truth. (1 John 3:17-18)

Reflection: Love, as an old movie title and Frank Sinatra song have it, truly is "a many splendored thing"! It has many levels, many meanings: the awakening of romance, the commitment of marriage or friendship, identification with others in compassion, a pervasive kindness toward others, the stirring of self-giving sacrifice, the pouring out of our hearts in prayer, the experience of mystical union. We all have many varied and wonderful experiences of love; and we all know the inevitable failures in love—our own and others.

Speaking of love, John begins with the basics. He finishes his statement that loving one another is the message we have heard from the beginning by asserting that we are to be "unlike Cain who belonged to the evil one and slaughtered his brother" (1 John 3:12a). In other words, love first of all means not killing each other. A good place to start!

But it is a skill we have not yet mastered! Even though our personal killing may not be of the fatal variety, most of us manage to send out a few poisoned arrows: little pricks that let someone know we do not think all that much of them. Even without words, our thoughts and attitudes can make for a destructive atmosphere that snuffs out life. In our efforts to counteract murder and war, we are called to start right at home with our own hearts and minds, replacing poisoned arrows with kind and forgiving thoughts and words.

Meditation: How are you being invited to love in deed and in truth today? Where around your house or in your neighbor's yard can you plant the seeds of love?

Prayer: God of simplicity and greatness, turn my attention away from unrealistic schemes for changing the world and open my eyes to the needs for love that are close at hand. Expand the narrowness of my heart so that the generosity of your love may touch my family, friends, neighbors, and coworkers today. I pray in the name of Jesus, Love incarnate. Amen.

God's Unconditional Love

Readings: 1 John 5:5-13; Mark 1:7-11 or Luke 3:23-38 or 3:23, 31-34, 36, 38

Scripture:
It happened in those days that Jesus came from Nazareth
    of Galilee
  and was baptized in the Jordan by John.
On coming up out of the water he saw the heavens being
    torn open
  and the Spirit, like a dove, descending upon him.
And a voice came from the heavens,
    "You are my beloved Son; with you I am well pleased."
    (Mark 1:9-11)

Reflection: Every child, no matter how old, longs to know the unconditional love of a parent. It is life's deepest security and the firm foundation for the healthy, self-giving love of adulthood.

About a month before her death at age ninety-five, with the help of my sister, my mother sent me a short note in her own shaky handwriting. Inserted among a few typical comments on daily life was this wonderful affirmation: "I love you. I am glad you are my child." These words touched me deeply, and the reality of the love they expressed carried me through many challenges. Reflecting on the power of this enduring maternal love has deepened my insight into the profound effect of Jesus' baptism, his realization that he is God's beloved Son.

Knowledge, in the depths of his being, that he was the beloved Son of God was the foundation for Jesus' desert endurance, his refusal to be dominated by earthly temptations (see Mark 1). The certainty of this knowledge, the experience of this love, was the foundation for all his choices, all his words, all his actions.

Although only God's love can be completely unconditional, all parental love mirrors and conveys that divine unconditional love of God for each human child. And even if a child is deprived of parental love because of life's unfortunate and even tragic circumstances, God's love never fails. God has sent and is sending Jesus into our world so that he can share with us through grace the Divine love that is his by nature.

Meditation: In what ways have you experienced the unconditional love of God for you?

Prayer: Beloved Son of God, you are dwelling within us and our world, pouring out God's unconditional love. Open our minds to this truth and our hearts and wills to this reality so that rooted and grounded in you, we may serve you and one another in generosity and joy. Amen.

January 7

Mary and the Wine

Readings: 1 John 5:14-21; John 2:1-11

Scripture:
There was a wedding at Cana in Galilee,
   and the mother of Jesus was there.
Jesus and his disciples were also invited to the wedding.
When the wine ran short,
   the mother of Jesus said to him,
   "They have no wine." (John 2:1-3)

Reflection: When the wine ran short in Cana at the wedding of the friends of Jesus and his mother, it was she, Mary, who noticed and wanted to prevent their embarrassment. How like a concerned woman friend she is, keenly attuned to the particulars of hospitality and the feelings and needs of her hosts!

John's Gospel, sometimes described as mystical in nature, is designed to draw its hearer and reader into the spiritual reality that lies beneath the surface of the text and the selected events that text describes. Actually all the Gospels are intended to do the same. The Gospel of John, however, heightens our awareness of this dynamic by singling out and designating seven special events as signs, plumbing their depths in the discourses that follow, and connecting them to *the* sign that gives meaning to them all, that is, the passion, death, and resurrection of Jesus. Though seemingly reluctant, at his mother's request, Jesus takes action! This miracle is more than an amazing feat, it is a sign that God's new covenant with humankind in Jesus fulfills the Mosaic covenant.

God's covenant with us in Jesus is our wedding feast. The festive wine is the Holy Spirit whose life in us is our richness, our joy. Jesus freely gives this wine to us filling us "to the brim" (John 2:7b) as we welcome his dying and rising in the particular circumstances of our lives. When due to lack of foresight or neglect—or even ill will—our wine jugs border on empty, would Mary not notice and intercede with her son for us? "She has no wine," "He has no wine," or "They have no wine" (John 2:3b), she would say. Trusting that her son will take action on our behalf if we truly long for the wine of the Holy Spirit, we celebrate this feast with joy.

Meditation: In what ways are you aware of a lack of wine, the absence of joy, in your spirit? Invite Mary into your presence and talk with her about what is missing.

Prayer: Mary, mother of Jesus, because of your intercession your son filled the water jars at Cana with wine. Pray for us now so that he may fill our hearts with the wine of his Holy Spirit. We pray this trusting in your concern for our need. Amen.

January 8: Solemnity of the Epiphany
(Roman Catholic Church)

Feast of the Baptism of the Lord
(Episcopal Church; see below, *January 9*)

God Made Manifest

Readings: Isa 60:1-6; Eph 3:2-3, 5-6; Matt 2:1-12

Scripture:
[B]ehold, magi from the east arrived in Jerusalem, saying,
"Where is the newborn king of the Jews?
We saw his star at its rising
and have come to do him homage." (Matt 2:1c-2)

Reflection: The multilayered theological and spiritual reality of the Epiphany comes to us in stories like the vignette in today's gospel reading. In every age we continue to mine its riches expressing them in art, poetry, and music.

Three magnificently dressed kings from the East arriving at a stable sheltering a mature, sturdy, common man watching over a serenely beautiful young woman dandling on her lap a child who is all light reaching out to his royal visitors! Such an image of the Epiphany has permeated our consciousness from early childhood by way of the various popular and classical depictions to which we have been exposed. If we are familiar with Gian Carlo Menotti's opera, *Amahl and the Night Visitors,* in our mind's ear we might also